Sun Certified
Enterprise Architect for
J2EE™ Technology Study Guide

ISBN 0-13-044916-4

90000
9 790130 449169

Mark Cade
Simon Roberts

Sun Certified Enterprise Architect for J2EE™ Technology Study Guide

Sun Microsystems Press
A Prentice Hall Title

The publisher offers discounts on this book when ordered in bulk quantities.
For more information, contact Corporate Sales Department, Prentice Hall PTR ,
One Lake Street, Upper Saddle River, NJ 07458. Phone: 800-382-3419; FAX: 201- 236-7141.
E-mail: corpsales@prenhall.com.

Editorial/production supervision: *Kathleen M. Caren*

Cover design director: *Jerry Votta*

Cover designer: *Anthony Gemmellaro*

Manufacturing manager: *Alexis R. Heydt-Long*

Marketing manager: *Debby vanDijk*

Acquisitions editor: *Gregory G. Doench*

Associate editor: *Eileen Clark*

Editorial assistant: *Brandt Kenna*

Sun Microsystems Press Publisher: *Michael Llwyd Alread*

14 15

ISBN 0-13-044916-4

Sun Microsystems Press
A Prentice Hall Title

CONTENTS

CHAPTER   5

Security   *91*

C H A P T E R   6

Internationalization   *127*

APPENDIX   A

PREFACE

Why We Wrote This Book

Sun certification exams are not tests given after class. If they were, it's unlikely that they would receive the wide ranging industry recognition that they enjoy. These exams are hard, and being hard means that they prove something, and that makes them worth passing. Not everybody does pass, even after repeated attempts.

The Sun exams are probably unique in that you don't have to take Sun training to pass, although of course, Sun training is helpful and a good idea to do anyway. The Sun exams have wide-ranging objectives that don't relate to one particular training course. The objectives for the Sun Certified Enterprise Architect (SCEA) for the Java 2 Platform, Enterprise Edition Technology exam are broad; they attempt to capture the main ideas that would be learned over a number of years as a computing professional, typically in a career that spans a longer time frame and more languages than just Java technology.

To address these issues, Sun's certification division plans to provide a study guide for each of its tests. This is one of those guides. This book is probably not the only study guide available for the exam, and it's certainly not the only way to prepare for the exam; however, we hope you'll find it helpful and that you'll learn something of value for your professional development, not just how to answer the exam questions. After all, the exam is meant to give you the opportunity to be a better architect, which in the long term will be far more helpful to your career than a piece of paper saying you passed an exam.

About the Authors

Between us, we have over ten years experience working with Java technology, in terms of developing systems, teaching, and working on the certification exams. We have considerably more experience in the pre-Java technology world of computing, including C, C++, machine languages, hardware design, networking with Transmission Control Protocol/Internet Protocol (TCP/IP), netbios and Novell, and database technologies. We were privileged to be members of the team that developed the architect certification exam, so we have an intimate knowledge of the difficulty of writing questions for this huge topic, and a fairly accurate view of the nature and scope of the exam. We don't claim to know it all, we don't think anyone does, this topic is too large. However, we hope that we have enough background knowledge, enough experience, and the right communication skills, to help you pass the architect certification exam, and to help you realize your potential as an architect.

We believe that whatever study method you use, and whatever resources you use to help you, the knowledge you gain will help you build better systems, and thereby become more successful in your work. We became involved in the exam project because we enjoy the thrill of creating a really elegant and successful system, and we wanted to help others experience that same satisfaction. For the same reason, we decided to take on the project that resulted in the book you're now reading.

About This Book

The SCEA exam is intended for seasoned computing personnel, and it is not possible to condense all the required knowledge into a single book. This book is a study guide. We've tried to cover the key facts tested in the exam, but you must understand the concepts as well as the facts to pass this exam. You should probably do additional reading, and you must develop a general understanding of the ideas tested in the exam.

Some of the exam questions might look at a particular issue from a slightly different perspective than the one presented in this book. That is why it is important that you understand the issues. We deliberately avoided giving you the answers to any questions, which would only devalue the exam. Furthermore, the exam is the subject of ongoing development, with new questions being added and old ones being removed. It's probably obvious that this is done to reduce the chance of cheating, which again would devalue the exam and thereby devalue the effort you put into passing it.

Given that this book doesn't just list the answers, what does it do? It introduces the key concepts covered in the exam and clarifies the terminology. This will ensure that you're "on the same page" as the exam developers. It also lists references in which you can find additional discussion of topics that you might want to research. And, it provides self-evaluation questions that are designed to help you determine if you understand the topic.

You might be surprised to know that you could disagree with some of the answers given in this book and not be wrong. Architecture depends on the interaction of a great many conflicting forces, and two experienced architects will often come to quite contradictory conclusions about how best to solve a particular problem.

Most of the questions in this book carefully enumerate the values of the customer, and, using these values as hints, you should be able to see why a particular answer is listed as correct. However, it's probably more important that you can see the relationship between the correct answers and the alternative answers.

In the multiple choice element of the exam there is only one acceptable answer (or combination of answers). Because of this, you must have the ability to evaluate the questions dispassionately. You must answer them based solely on the information provided, and you should avoid the tendency to fill in additional "ifs, buts, and wherefores." Often the real exam lists a possible answer that is perfectly reasonable if you include just one additional value judgement, but because that value judgement is unsupported by the question, the answer is wrong in the context of the exam.

Learning to think like this isn't just a skill for getting through the exam, it will help you in your profession because it allows you to evaluate your own decision-making process, and determine if you are applying your own secret values to a decision, or if you are actually responding to a stated customer requirement. If you are an experienced architect, you know that it's OK, even essential in many cases, to use your values to fill in the blanks left by the customer. However, when you do so, you owe it to your customer to communicate your ideas. You might just prompt them to remember additional information.

Who Should Read This Book

This book is not intended to give a novice programmer the skills and knowledge needed to pass the exam. It is intended to help complete the knowledge of someone who has several years of computing experience, although not all of that must be using Java technology; in fact you're probably better equipped if you have used other technologies as well. You should be aware of the broad meaning of the technologies discussed, but you do not necessarily have to have experience using all of them.

As we wrote the book, we used the following profile as a guide for the type of reader that might find this book helpful.

- You understand object-oriented concepts, such as encapsulation, inheritance, and polymorphism, and you're comfortable with the interfaces as used in the Java programming language.

- You have programmed in an object-oriented language, probably the Java programming language.

- You have designed object-oriented systems.

- You are preparing for the "Sun Certified Enterprise Architect for the Java 2 Platform, Enterprise Edition" exam or are otherwise seeking to improve your skills as an architect.

There are certainly other profiles for whom this book will be valuable. For example, many managers would find this book useful, provided they have a reasonably technical background, and they will gain sufficient understanding of the processes and values of architecture to allow them to manage effectively.

How This Book Is Organized

The chapters in this book describe either general topics covered in the exam or one of the key objective groupings of the multiple choice part of the exam. Some of the general chapters provide overall background information and skills, and some relate directly to the assignment.

The chapters that relate directly to exam objectives take a consistent form. They start with a description of the objectives and provide background information about the topic. Next is a description of the prerequisite information that we assume you already know. Be careful about these prerequisites, we've tried to keep them to a minimum, and in some cases, there is no prior knowledge assumed, but if there are prerequisites listed, you must ensure that you meet all the prerequisites. After the prerequisite list, the chapters move into the body of the discussion. At this point, you'll find the main descriptions of the issues at hand.

After a discussion of the issues, this book reviews the key points contained in the chapter. This will help you learn and review the material because it is a concise listing as opposed to the in-depth description provided in the chapter. If you believe that you already understand the issues in a chapter, you can simply go directly to this list and see if you are familiar with the information in the list.

Finally, the chapter presents a number of self-evaluation questions. You should not look at these questions as sample exam questions, although some do take the same format. Generally, they are intended to make you think, and to probe your understanding of the topic. This is much easier to achieve using a broad-based question rather than the more precise exam questions. You should be less concerned about the answers matching your answer, and more concerned about your thought processes covering the same ideas as are discussed in the question. As an example, this book contains questions that use a free-form answer, such as, "what are the issues that would influence a decision about..." You won't see that type of question in the exam, although you will need to outline your decision-making processes and priorities in your assignment submission. When you work through a question of this type, you should get a feeling of "OK, I thought of all those issues" and a feeling of confidence that you understand all of these issues. If you missed something, or if you don't really feel you understand a particular topic, you should be honest with yourself. Taking an honest, professional attitude to your self-judgement is the only way you can get the best from yourself and from this book.

About the Case Study

This book presents a case study in a format that is similar to the assignment. You are presented with use cases, a domain object model, and additional requirements. This format should be familiar to you as an architect. Every system you work on in the real world will have requirements of some sort and it just so happens the exam assignment has chosen to define the requirements in use cases and a domain object model. As the architect for the system, you must provide class diagram(s), component diagram(s), and sequence or collaboration diagrams to communicate your architecture.

About the Exam

The exam has three parts, a multiple choice test, an assignment, and a written part in which you discuss specific parts of your assignment.

Acknowledgments

Mark Cade wishes to thank his family, wife Lara, son Alec and daughter Sara. Without your support this book would not have been possible. I hope you will let me back into the family, remember, I'm the guy in the basement typing away.

Simon Roberts wishes to thank Solveig for her energetic support, my children, Emily and Bethan, for my purpose (and for staying asleep long enough to allow my early morning writing sessions to be productive), my flight instructors for putting up with my strange hours, and all my friends for their encouragement.

We would like to thank the people who have provided insight and reviewed the book: John Walsh, Brian Cook, Robert Pittman, Chris Steel, Alan Blackwell, Charlie Martin, Mark Cao, Nick Wilde and the Sun Java Center e-mail list for the many wonderful discussions.

We would especially like to thank Patricia Parkhill, our friend, technical writer, and editor for helping us become better writers and putting up with us. Pat, thanks for all the long hours and tedious work on the book; without you this book would have never been completed.

What Is Architecture?

Each chapter in this book follows the same basic structure. The chapter starts with a listing of the exam objectives that are described in the chapter. This is followed by either an "Introduction" section or a "Prerequisite Review" section, which identifies any assumed knowledge for the chapter. A "Discussion" section, which describes the topics in the chapter with a focus on the objectives is next. This is followed by "Essential Points," which is a summary of the key ideas in the chapter. Finally the "Review Your Progress" section focuses on questions that might appear on the exam.

After completing this chapter, you will be able to meet the following J2EE technology architect exam objectives:

- Role of the architect
- Service-level requirements

Introduction

There are many different definitions of the word architecture. Webster's definition is "the art or science of building." Webster's computer industry definition of architecture is "the manner in which the components of a computer or computer system are arranged and integrated." This chapter presents a variation of Webster's definition of architecture with the remainder of the book re-enforcing this definition.

Creating an architecture to build a system has increased ten-fold in the last couple of years, due to the growth of the Internet. Before the Internet explosion, an architect created an architecture to handle the internal users of the company, which could number in the hundreds. However, the Internet has opened a company's computing resources to their customers, which means the architect must now create a system architecture that can handle thousands of users with unpredictable usage patterns. If your systems do not perform and meet the expectations of the customers, then these customers will find other companies with systems that can handle their expectations. Therefore, the architectures you create can have a direct impact on your company's bottom line.

Prerequisite Review

In an attempt to keep this book from getting larger than the dictionary, it assumes a certain level of knowledge for the readers. If you do not have the prerequisite knowledge, you must gain this knowledge elsewhere before proceeding with this book. This book assumes the following prerequisites:

- You understand object-oriented concepts, such as encapsulation, inheritance, polymorphism, and interfaces.
- You have programmed in an objected-oriented language, preferably the Java programming language.
- You have designed object-oriented programs and systems.
- You are using this book to prepare for the Sun Certified Enterprise Architect (SCEA) for Java 2 Platform, Enterprise Edition Technology exam.

Becoming a full-fledged system architect requires many years of real world experience creating architectures and designing systems. This book will provide you with the knowledge you need to start gaining that valuable experience, as well as prepare you to become a Sun Certified Enterprise Architect for Java 2 Platform, Enterprise Edition (J2EE) technology.

Discussion

The best starting point for this book, is to make sure you are on the same page as the exam developers. Having this common vocabulary will reduce confusion in the later chapters. A clear and concise definition of architecture is imperative to your success on this exam. Once you understand the definition, you must understand your role in creating an architecture. You must realize what your tasks are. Finally, you must understand the purpose of creating an architecture. You create an architecture to support the service-level requirements of a system. Without service-level requirements, your systems cannot meet customer demand for availability, reliability, and scalability. It is these service-level requirements that keep a company from having a "CNN" moment, which occurs when the failure of your computer systems makes headline news on CNN.

1.1 Understanding Architecture

According to the Rational Unified Process:

"Software architecture encompasses the significant decisions about the organization of a software system. The selection of the structural elements and their interfaces by which the system is composed together with their behavior as specified in the collaboration among those elements. The composition of the structural and behavioral elements into progressively larger subsystems, the architectural style that guides this organization, these elements, and their interfaces, their collaborations, and their composition. Software architecture is concerned not only with structure and behavior but also with usage, functionality, performance, resilience, reuse, comprehensibility, economic and technology constraints and trade-offs, and aesthetic issues."[1]

That is a pretty lengthy definition, so let's look at a little simpler definition provided by the SunTone Architecture Methodology:

Architecture is a set of structuring principles that enables a system to be comprised of a set of simpler systems each with its own local context that is independent of but not inconsistent with the context of the larger system as a whole.[2]

---

1. Unified Process: An Introduction
2. Sun Microsystems, Inc.

Both definitions focus on system structure. You create an architecture to describe the structure of the system to be built and how that structure supports the business and service-level requirements. You can define the structure of a system as the mechanisms that the system employs to solve the common problems of the system. A mechanism is a capability that supports the business requirements in a consistent and uniform manner. For example, persistence is a mechanism that should be used consistently throughout the system. This means that any time the system uses persistence, it is handled in the same manner. By defining persistence as an architectural mechanism, you provide a default method of addressing persistence that all designers should follow and implement consistently. The architectural mechanisms, such as persistence, distribution, communication, transaction management, and security are the infrastructure on which you build the system and must be defined in your architecture.

What does it mean to create an architecture? It means that you have created a software infrastructure that addresses the service-level requirements that have been identified for the system. For example, if the system has a service-level requirement that states no user response time will be greater than three seconds, then the software infrastructure you create must ensure that the system can meet this requirement. It also means that you have given the designers an infrastructure that allows them to design and code the system without worrying about compromising this service-level requirement. One of the real issues around architecture is: When does the creation of an architecture stop and the design process begin? There is not a definitive answer for every system. This issue of architecture and design can be summed up in terms of focus and control. Architecture defines what is going to be built and design outlines how you will build it. Architecture is controlled by one or a few individuals who focus on a big picture and design is controlled by many individuals who focus on the details of how to achieve the big picture. An architect creates an architecture to a point where the design team can use it to make the system achieve its overall goals. So, if you are creating an architecture for experienced designers, you might not produce the detail that you would need if you had a group of less experienced designers.

As you create an architecture to satisfy the business and service-level requirements of a system, you usually don't have unlimited funds to purchase hardware, software and development resources, so you need to make the system work within your predefined limitations. For example, how can you make the system scale to meet the demands of the Internet age, when you have only a single computer to support your internal employees? How do you create an architecture without funds to buy software products? These are examples of problems faced by architects when they are creating a system architecture. You will be presented with many difficult choices and make many trade-offs to solve these types of problems. As you make these trade-offs, it is important that you document each decision made regarding the architecture of the system. If you make a decision to have an Oracle database persist the objects in the system, then you should document why you chose Oracle over another database vendor. This allows others working on the project or entering the project at a later time to understand why decisions were made and prevents you from justifying your decision over and over again. Most of the trade-offs you make when creating an architecture focus on the service-level requirements or mechanisms. Most systems do not have the funding available to meet all of the service-level requirements originally envisioned by the system stakeholders. So, you as the architect must balance the service-level requirements against the cost to attain these requirements. If it will cost your entire budget to buy high-availability hardware to achieve the 24x7 availability, thereby leaving no money to purchase an application server to help maintain that service-level requirement on the software side, you must make adjustments in your software architecture. These adjustments depend on the system for which you are creating the architecture and your relationship with the stakeholders.

1.2 Role of the Architect

"The ideal architect should be a person of letters, a mathematician, familiar with historical studies, a diligent student of philosophy, acquainted with music, not ignorant of medicine, learned in the responses of jurisconsults, familiar with astronomy and astronomical calculations."—*Vitruvius, circa 25 BC*

Vitruvius was not referring to a software architect, but the basic idea is that the architect should have the following characteristics. An architect should be a person who is well-rounded, mature, experienced, educated, learns quickly, a leader, communicates well and can make the difficult decision when necessary. For architects to be well-rounded, they must have a working knowledge of the business or problem domain. They can gain this knowledge through experience or education. In addition, architects must have a broad knowledge of technology. An architect might have first-hand experience with a particular technology, but they must have at least a general understanding of competing technologies to make informed decisions about which technology can work best. A good architect evaluates all possible solutions to a problem regardless of the technology being used.

What does the architect do? What is the difference between an architect compared with a senior developer? These are some of the common questions asked. The designer is concerned with what happens when a user presses a button and the architect is concerned with what happens when ten thousand users press a button. An architect mitigates the technical risks associated with a system. A technical risk is something that is unknown, unproven, or untested. Risks are usually associated with the service-level requirements and can occasionally be associated with a business requirement. Regardless of the type of risk, it is easier to address the risks early in the project while creating an architecture, then to wait until construction when you have a large developer base that could potentially be waiting while risks are solved.

An architect must lead the development team to ensure the designers and developers build the system according to the architecture. As the leader, difficult decisions must be made about trade-offs in the system and the architect is the person who must make those decisions. To lead, the architect must be a good written and oral communicator. It is up to the architect to communicate the system to the designers and developers who will build it. This is typically done with visual models and group discussions. If the architect cannot communicate effectively, then the designers and developers will probably not build the system correctly.

1.3 Service-level Requirements

In addition to the business requirements of a system, you must satisfy the service-level or quality of service (QoS) requirements. As an architect, it is your job to work with the stakeholders of the system during the inception and elaboration phases to define a quality of service measurement for each of the service-level requirements. The architecture you create must address the following service-level requirements: performance, scalability, reliability, availability, extensibility, maintainability, manageability, and security. You will have to make trade-offs between these requirements. For example, if the most important service-level requirement is the performance of the system, you might sacrifice the maintainability and extensibility of the system to ensure that you meet the performance quality of service. As the expanding Internet opens more computing opportunities, the service-level requirements are becoming increasingly important as the users of these Internet systems are no longer just the company employees, but they are now the company's customers.

Performance

The performance requirement is usually measured in terms of response time for a given screen transaction per user. In addition to response time, performance can also be measured in transaction throughput, which is the number of transactions in a given time period, usually one second. For example, you could have a performance measurement that could be no more than three seconds for each screen form or a transaction throughput of one hundred transactions in one second. Regardless of the measurement, you need to create an architecture that allows the designers and developers to complete the system without considering the performance measurement.

Scalability

Scalability is the ability to support the required quality of service as the system load increases without changing the system. A system can be considered scalable if, as the load increases, the system still responds within the acceptable limits. It might be that you have a performance measurement of a response time between two and five seconds. If the system load increases and the system can maintain the performance quality of service of less than a five second response time, then your system is scalable. To understand scalability, you must first understand the capacity of a system, which is defined as the maximum number of processes or users a system can handle and still maintain the quality of service. If a system is running at capacity and can no longer respond within an acceptable time frame, then it has reached its maximum scalability. To scale a system that has met capacity, you must add additional hardware. This additional hardware can be added vertically or horizontally. Vertical scaling involves adding additional processors, memory, or disks to the current machine(s). Horizontal scaling involves adding more machines to the environment, thus increasing the overall system capacity. The architecture you create must be able to handle the vertical or horizontal scaling of the hardware. Vertical scaling of a software architecture is easier than the horizontal scaling. Why? Adding more processors or memory typically does not have an impact on your architecture, but having your architecture run on multiple machines and still appear to be one system is more difficult. The remainder of this book describes ways you can make your system scale horizontally.

Reliability

Reliability ensures the integrity and consistency of the application and all its transactions. As the load increases on your system, your system must continue to process requests and handle transactions as accurately as it did before the load increased. Reliability can have a negative impact on scalability. If the system cannot maintain the reliability as the load increases, then the system is really not scalable. So, for a system to truly scale it must be reliable.

Availability

Availability ensures that a service/resource is always accessible. Reliability can contribute to availability, but availability can be achieved even if components fail. By setting up an environment of redundant components and failover, an individual component can fail and have a negative impact on reliability, but the service is still available due to the redundancy.

Extensibility

Extensibility is the ability to add additional functionality or modify existing functionality without impacting existing system functionality. You cannot measure extensibility when the system is deployed, but it shows up the first time you must extend the functionality of the system. You should consider the following when you create the architecture and design to help ensure extensibility: low coupling, interfaces, and encapsulation.

Maintainability

Maintainability is the ability to correct flaws in the existing functionality without impacting other components of the system. This is another of those systemic qualities that you cannot measure at the time of deployment. When creating an architecture and design, you should consider the following to enhance the maintainability of a system: low coupling, modularity, and documentation.

Manageability

Manageability is the ability to manage the system to ensure the continued health of a system with respect to scalability, reliability, availability, performance, and security. Manageability deals with system monitoring of the QoS requirements and the ability to change the system configuration to improve the QoS dynamically without changing the system. Your architecture must have the ability to monitor the system and allow for dynamic system configuration.

Security

Security is the ability to ensure that the system cannot be compromised. Security is by far the most difficult systemic quality to address. Security includes not only issues of confidentiality and integrity, but also relates to Denial-of-Service (DoS) attacks that impact availability. Creating an architecture that is separated into functional components makes it easier to secure the system because you can build security zones around the components. If a component is compromised, then it is easier to contain the security violation to that component.

Essential Points

Architecture is a set of structuring principles that enables a system to be comprised of a set of simpler systems each with its own local context that is independent of but not inconsistent with the context of the larger system as a whole. [3]

- The role of the architect is to make designer and developers productive as quickly as possible.
- Creating an architecture to address the service-level requirements will help you to avoid that "CNN" moment.
- Scalability is the ability to support the required quality of service as the system load increases without changing the system.
- Reliability ensures the integrity and consistency of the application and all of its transactions.
- Availability ensures that a service/resource is always accessible.

---

3. Sun Microsystems, Inc.

- Extensibility is the ability to add additional functionality or modify existing functionality without impacting existing system functionality.
- Maintainability is the ability to correct flaws in the existing functionality without impacting other components of the system.
- Manageability is the ability to manage the system to ensure the continued health of a system with respect to scalability, reliability, availability, performance, and security.
- Security is the ability to ensure that the system cannot be compromised.

▼ Review Your Progress

This chapter lays the ground work for the rest of this book, so there are no specific questions to ask.

J2EE Overview

The Java 2 Platform, Enterprise Edition (J2EE) is Sun Microsystems distributed computing framework. It is this framework that is the basis for the exam.

After completing this chapter, you will be able to meet the following J2EE technology architect exam objectives:

- Select, from a list, the application aspects that are suited for implementation using J2EE
- Identify suitable J2EE technologies for the implementation of specified application aspects
- Select, from a list, those application aspects that are suited to implementation using EJB
- List the required classes/interfaces that must be provided for an EJB
- Distinguish between Session and Entity beans.
- Recognize appropriate uses for Entity, Stateful Session, and Stateless Session beans
- Distinguish between stateful and stateless Session beans
- Explain how the EJB container does life cycle management and has the capability to increase scalability

- State the benefits of bean pooling in an EJB container
- State the benefits of Passivation in an EJB container
- State the transactional behavior in a given scenario for an enterprise bean method with a specified transactional attributed as defined in the deployment descriptor
- State the benefits and costs of container-managed persistence
- Identify costs and benefits of using an intermediate data-access object between an entity bean and the data resource.

Prerequisite Review

This chapter assumes that you have a basic understanding of J2EE. You are not expected to program to the APIs of J2EE, but you are expected to understand the capabilities of the APIs. This chapter does not describe J2EE in detail. It describes those aspects of J2EE that are tested in the exam.

Discussion

J2EE is a platform for developing distributed enterprise software applications. J2EE consists of the following (known as the J2EE Framework):

- J2EE Platform – A standard platform for hosting J2EE applications.
- Reference Implementation – An application server that supports the latest specification, except its focus is on the most recent release of the specification and it is not production ready.
- Compatibility Test Suite – A utility that verifies that an application server is compatible with J2EE. Without the Compatibility Test Suite, each vendor could interpret and implement the specification differently, thereby reducing the benefit of the write once, run anywhere functionality in the J2EE platform.
- Application Programming Model (APM) Blueprint – A reference provided to teach individuals how to develop distributed applications using J2EE. In the last year, the APM has lost some of its usefulness as more people become familiar with developing distributed applications and more books and training classes are available.

2.1 Implementing Applications Using J2EE

The J2EE Framework allows you to develop distributed applications by providing a set of basic services around transaction management, security checks, state management, and resource management. It is the application server that provides the actual implementation of the J2EE Framework. Prior to the application server, each company and sometimes each system developed the basic distributed applications services of transactions, security and persistence.

2.2 The J2EE APIs

The following list describes the technologies used by J2EE to implement parts of a distributed computing application:

- Java 2 Standard Edition (J2SE)
- Java Database Connectivity (JDBC) – A standard API used to connect the Java platform to database resources in a vendor-independent manner.
- RMI-JRMP – Remote Method Invocation (RMI) that uses the Java Remote Message Protocol (JRMP).
- Java Interface Definition Language (Java IDL) – A service that incorporates Common Object Request Broker Architecture (CORBA) into the Java platform to provide interoperability using standard Interface Definition Language (IDL) defined by the Object Management Group (OMG).
- Remote Method Invocation-Internet Inter-ORB Protocol (RMI-IIOP) – Protocol that enables RMI programmers to combine the benefits of using the RMI APIs and CORBA IIOP communications protocol to communicate with CORBA-compliant clients that have been developed using any language compliant with CORBA.
- Enterprise JavaBeans (EJB) – A component architecture for the development and deployment of component-based distributed business applications.
- Servlets – Interact with a Web client in a request-response mechanism. This mechanism is based on behavior of the HTTP.
- JavaServer Pages (JSP) – Used for building applications containing dynamic Web content, such as HyperText Markup Language

(HTML), Dynamic HyperText Markup Language (DHTML), and eXtensible Markup Language (XML).

- Java Message Server (JMS) – An API to communicate with Message Oriented Middleware (MOM) to enable point-to-point and publish/subscribe messaging between systems.
- Java Naming and Directory Interface (JNDI) – A unified interface to access different types of naming and directory services.
- Java Transaction API (JTA) – A set of APIs that allows transaction management. Applications can use the JTA APIs to start, commit, and abort transactions.
- JavaMail – An API that provides a platform-independent and protocol-independent framework to build mail and messaging applications.
- JavaBeans Activation Framework (JAF) – API for an activation framework that is used by other packages, such as JavaMail. You can use JAF to determine the type of data, encapsulate access to that data, discover the operations available on that data, and instantiate the appropriate bean to perform these operations. For example, JavaMail uses JAF to determine what object to instantiate based on the mime type of the object.

2.3 Components of J2EE

J2EE is built on a component container model. The four core container components provide runtime support for the J2EE components by means of APIs. These core components relate to the four types of containers supported in J2EE, which are Application Client, Applet, Web, and EJB. The following are the core application components supported by J2EE:

- The Java application – The Java application components are standalone programs than run inside the Application Client container. The Application Client container provides the APIs to support messaging, remote invocation, database connectivity and lookup services. The following APIs are required for the Application Client container: J2SE, JMS, JNDI, RMI-11OP, and JDBC. This container is provided by the application server vendors.

- Applets – Applet components are Java applets that run in the Applet container, which is the basic browser that supports the Java technology. The Applet must support the J2SE APIs.

- Servlets and JSPs – Servlet and JSP components are Web-based components that run in the Web container, which is supported by a Web server. The Web container is the run-time execution environment for JSPs and servlets. The Web container must support the following APIs: J2SE, JMS, JNDI, JTA, JavaMail, JAF, RMI-IIOP, and JDBC. JSPs and servlets provide a mechanism for dynamic content preparation, processing and formatting related to presentation.

- Enterprise JavaBeans (EJB) – EJB components are business components that run in the EJB container. The EJB components are the core of a J2EE application. The EJB container provides transaction management, state management, resource pooling, and security checks. The EJB container must support the following APIs: J2SE, JMS, JNDI, JTA, JavaMail, JAF, RMI-IIOP, and JDBC. Because EJB components are the core of J2EE, most exam questions are related in some way to EJB. Therefore, the majority of this chapter describes different components and functions of EJB.

2.4 Using EJB

EJB should contain the business logic for the application, so it is no surprise that EJB is the heart of most applications. An enterprise bean has the following characteristics:

- Contains business logic that operates on enterprise data

- Created and managed by a container

- Mediates client access

- Contains metadata, such as transaction and security attributes, separate from the bean

- Provides transaction management, state management, resource pooling, and security checks. If you have an application that does not require security and/or transaction support, then you must really question whether you should use EJB.

2.5 Specifying Classes and Interfaces for EJB

To keep some consistency for EJB, each EJB must have the following interfaces and class:

- The home interface is developed by the bean developer. The Application server provides an implementation for this interface. The home interface should extend javax.ejb.EJBHome. The home interface acts as a factory pattern to create instances of the EJB. It also allows the client to create, remove, or find an EJB.

- The remote interface is developed by the bean developer and the Application server provides an implementation. It should extend javax.ejb.EJBObject. The remote interface contains the business methods that can be called by the client. The remote interface acts as a proxy.

- The bean class is developed by the bean developer and contains the implementation of the method defined in the remote interface. It should extend javax.ejb.SessionBean or javax.ejb.EntityBean.

Figure 2–1 illustrates the classes and interfaces for EJB.

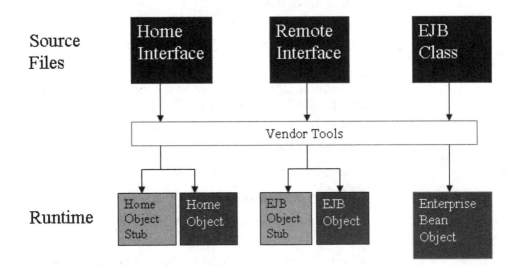

Figure 2–1 *Classes and Interfaces for EJB*

2.6 Using Session and Entity Beans

Enterprise applications require flexible components in the business logic. Components must provide stateless services, provide conversational state, and support the sharing of enterprise data. Enterprise Java-Beans (EJB) provides two basic types of beans to support the different components required in an enterprise application: session and entity. Entity beans provide for the persistence and sharing of enterprise data in a J2EE application. This is not to say that a session bean could not persist an object, but the entity bean specializes in persisting objects. Session beans provide the business logic and workflow associated with the J2EE application, which corresponds to the stateless services and conversational services.

2.7 Stateless and Stateful Session Beans

There are two types of session beans: stateless and stateful.

Stateless Beans

Stateless session beans do not hold any conversational state for a client. However, this does not mean they cannot hold a state. Stateless session beans can hold a state, but the state is not guaranteed to be specific to the calling client. This means you can use stateless session beans to do almost anything in your application.

Stateful Session Beans

Stateful session beans give you the capability to hold a conversational state for a client. There are any number of ways to handle a conversational state in an enterprise application, but if the state needs to be close to the business logic, then it should be in a stateful session bean. A shopping cart is an example of a stateful session bean.

2.8 EJB Life Cycle

Each EJB has a unique life cycle. This life cycle dictates the behavior of the EJB. If you use the appropriate EJB, then it is the life cycle of the EJB that can help the scalability of an application.

Figure 2–2 illustrates the life cycle of a stateless session bean.

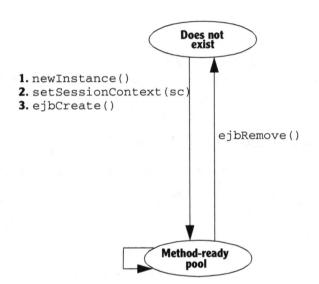

Figure 2–2 *Life Cycle of a Stateless Session Bean*

1. If the bean does not exist, the container invokes the `newInstance()` method on the bean class, which starts the life cycle.
2. The container calls the `setSessionContext()` method and then calls the `ejbCreate()` method. The bean instance is now in the method-ready pool and waiting for a business method call from any client.
3. When the container no longer needs the instance, the container invokes the `ejbRemove()` method, which removes the instance of the session bean

Figure 2–3 illustrates the life cycle of a stateful session bean.

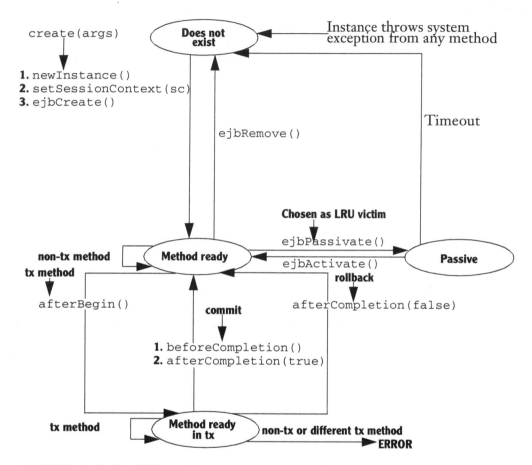

Figure 2–3 *Life Cycle of a Stateful Session Bean*

1. The client invokes a `create(args)` method on home interface.
2. The container invokes the `newInstance()` method on the bean.
3. The bean, calls the `setSessionContext()` method and the `ejbCreate()` method on the instance and returns the EJB object reference to the client. The instance of the stateful bean is ready to accept business methods.
4. Based on the transaction context, the stateful bean invokes the method with either the `tx` method or non-`tx` method. Nontransactional methods are executed while the bean is in a ready state. The invocation of the transactional method causes the instance to be included in transaction. The container issues the `afterBegin()` method on the instance of the bean.

5. If a transaction commit has been requested, the transaction service notifies the container, which issues a `beforeCompletion` method on the bean instance.

6. The transaction service attempts to commit the transaction, resulting in either a commit or rollback.

7. When the transaction is complete, the container issues the `afterCompletion()` method on the bean instance specifying the status of completion as either commit or rollback. If the status is rollback, the bean instance might need to restore the conversational state.

8. The container might decide that the bean instance should be evicted from memory. In this case, the container issues an `ejbPassivate()` method on the instance.

9. While in a passivated state, the container can remove the instance after a timeout has expired. If a client attempts to access the bean instance, the container throws a `java.rmi.NoSuchObjectException`.

10. If a client invokes a passivated bean instance that has not timed out, the container restores the instance's state from secondary storage and issues an `ejbActivate()` method. The bean instance is again ready for client methods.

11. When a client calls the `remove()` method on an EJB object, this causes the container to issue the `ejbRemove()` method on the bean.

The only time an application incurs the cost of creating a session bean is if one does not exist. If a bean already exists, then one is pulled from the method-ready pool, used and replaced when done. It is this pool of beans that improves the scalability of the application by being able to handle more requests with fewer resources.

2.9 Uses of Entity Beans, Stateful Beans, and Stateless Beans

Entity beans are used to persist the enterprise data. The entity bean is a sharable enterprise data object that can be used by many users concurrently.

The stateful session bean is used to manage the state of a users session on the server. An example of a stateful session bean would be a shopping cart. The stateless session bean can be used to implement the business logic and workflow of an application.

2.10 Managing EJB Using Bean Pooling

The container cannot handle an unlimited number of EJB, therefore the container must pool the resources and share them across users. Each EJB, when deployed, specifies the number of instances to pool and reuse. EJB are not lightweight objects that can be created and destroyed when necessary. They are heavy objects that take considerable resource to create and destory. Therefore, the application server will manage a pool of EJB that users can use throughout the application. By having this pool, the application server can handle more requests since it does not have to spend time creating and destroying objects.

2.11 Passivation of EJB

Passivation is the process of writing the bean's state to a file on the file system, so the instance of the bean can be used by another session. You use passivation to handle more requests with fewer resources. This is only available with entity and stateful session beans. With a stateless bean, you cannot use passivation because there is no state. When the passivation session returns, the bean is activated and the bean state is reloaded into an instance of the bean.

2.12 Using Transactions

Transactions are a big part of most enterprise applications. Transactions enable you to change your mind and return to a previous action (rollback) or go forward and commit the action. Without transactions, you cannot delete or change the work performed. A transaction must adhere to the ACID principal. It must be Atomic, Consistent, Isolatable, and Durable. Atomic means the transaction does not partially complete. It is either totally complete or it is backed out to where it started. A consistent transaction leaves the datastore in a consistent state. You can access the datastore and get the correct result. An isolatable transaction is independent of other transactions. The completion of your transaction does not depend on another transaction outside of your control. Durable transactions should survive a system failure. If the system fails in the middle of the transaction, then the system should back out the transaction for consistency and atomicity.

When you are creating a J2EE application, you must decide where the transaction demarcation should take place. For example, should the transaction start in a servlet and propagate to an EJB or should the transaction be fully contained in the EJB? You must also decide whether to have programmatic control or declarative control of the transaction. Programmatic control allows you to demarcate the start of a transaction. This equates to bean-managed transactions (BMTs). There is no difference in BMT and CMT when the transaction has been demarcated. Both methods use the same rollback and commit process. Declarative transaction support is handled by the container and does not require you to code the demarcation. Declarative control is used in container-managed transactions (CMTs). CMT allows the bean deployer to configure the bean at run time by modifying the transaction attributes for the bean methods. The transaction attribute defines the container's behavior when a client is invoking the bean method. The following describes the six attributes that cover all possible behaviors for transaction support on an EJB. Table 2.1 on page 23 gives a summary of the attributes.

- The Required attribute, means the container ensures that the method is invoked with a transaction. If the calling client does not have a transaction, then the container starts a transaction. If the calling client has a transaction, then the container passes the transaction to the method.

- The Requires New attribute means that the container always starts a new transaction when invoking this method. If the calling client has a transaction, the container suspends the transaction and starts a new one. This is not a nested transaction because the outcome of the new transaction has no impact on the suspended transaction. If the calling client does not have a transaction, then the container creates a new transaction and invokes the method.

- The Not Supported attribute means the method cannot handle a transaction. If the calling client has a transaction, then the container suspends the transaction before invoking the method. If the calling client does not have a transaction, the container invokes the method.

- The Supports attribute means the bean method accepts a transaction if available, but does not require the application server to create a new transaction. If the calling client has a transaction, the container propagates the transaction to the method. If the calling client does not have a transaction, then the container invokes the method.

- The Mandatory attribute states that the calling client must have a transaction. If the calling client has a transaction, the container propagates the transaction to the method. If the calling client does not have a transaction, then the container throws a `javax.transaction.TransactionRequiredException`.
- The Never attribute means that the bean is not expecting a transaction. If the calling client has a transaction, then the container throws `java.rmi.RemoteException`. If the calling client has no transaction, then the container just invokes the method.

Table 2.1 summarizes the behavior of the container for each of the transaction attributes.

Table 2.1 *Transaction Attributes*

TRANSACTION ATTRIBUTE	CALLING CLIENT HAS TRANSACTION	CALLING CLIENT DOES NOT HAVE TRANSACTION
Required	Transaction Propagated	New Transaction Started
Requires New	Transaction suspended, then new transaction is started	New transaction started
Not Supported	Transaction suspended	
Supports	Transaction propagated	
Mandatory	Transaction propagated	Throws `javax.transaction.TransactionRequired Exception`
Never	Throws `java.rmi.RemoteException`	

2.13 Using Container-Managed Persistence

There are two ways an entity bean can persist the object, container-managed persistence (CMP) or bean-managed persistence (BMP). In CMP, the container handles the implementation of the code necessary to insert, read, and update an object in a data source. In BMP, the application developer creates the implementation for the insert, read, and update of an object. CMP is the ideal way to develop an application because it requires less code changes by the application developer when the data model changes. However, to provide this flexibility, CMP does not generate the most efficient SQL queries.

Unfortunately, the object relational mapping tools are still maturing. As the tools mature, you should use BMP with data access objects (DAO).

2.14 Using Intermediate Data-Access Objects

If you decide that BMP is the best approach for your entity beans, then this means you are coding the SQL into your entity beans. It's an attempt to reduce the coupling of the entity beans with the SQL necessary to read, insert, update and delete an object, create a DAO that encapsulates the SQL. By encapsulating the code necessary to read, insert, update and delete an object you have reduced your dependency on code and data changes.

The DAO contains the implementation code to insert, update, delete, and read an object in a data source. This allows an entity bean to be defined as BMP, but the entity bean can change to CMP when the tools are better suited to handle the CMP. Encapsulating the data access into the DAO instead of the entity bean allows for the bean to replace the DAO with the CMP support from the container.

The cost of using DAOs is the additional layer and overhead of creating and garbage collection of the DAO. In addition, if you are not experienced with writing SQL code, then you could be writing slow running SQL commands.

Essential Points

The following summarizes the most important points described in this chapter:

- Applications that are distributed and require transactions, security, and resource management are suitable for implementation using J2EE technology.
- JSP and servlets are well suited to implement the user component aspect of a J2EE application.
- EJBs are suited to the implementation of business logic in a J2EE application.
- Application aspects that are suited to implementation using EJB are persistence, transaction, support, and security.

- The classes required to implement an EJB are: `javax.ejb.EJBHome`, `javax.ejb.EJBObject`, and your method implementations using either `javax.ejb.SessionBean` or `javax.ejb.EntityBean`.
- Entity beans are a shared resource that is persisted and session beans are associated with a user request and are not shared.
- Stateful session beans maintain a user's conversational state whereas a stateless session bean is shared among many users and each user controls the bean for a single request/response.
- Bean pooling allows for more users to use the system with fewer resources.
- Passivation allows the EJB container to use fewer stateful session beans to support more requests.
- CMP allows you to create persisted objects without having to write and maintain the code to persist the object. The down side to CMP is that the tools are not mature enough to provide the performance necessary for an enterprise application.
- DAOs allow you to control the access of data from resources and switch to CMP when the tools have better support, but this means you must write and maintain the SQL code.

▼ Review Your Progress

This section reviews the objectives described in the chapter and provides review questions to ensure that you understand the important points in the chapter.

OBJECTIVE: SELECT, FROM A LIST, THE APPLICATION ASPECTS THAT ARE SUITED FOR IMPLEMENTATION USING J2EE

1. Which of the following is not an application aspect suited for J2EE?
   A. Transactions
   B. Applet
   C. Security
   D. Resource management
   E. Distributed

Objective: Identify suitable J2EE technologies for the implementation of specified application aspects

2. *Which technology would you use to implement asynchronous messages within J2EE?*
    A. JMS
    B. RMI
    C. JNDI
    D. HTTP

Objective: Select, from a list, those application aspects that are suited to implementation using EJB

3. *Which is not an application aspect suited to implementation using EJB?*
    A. Distribution
    B. Security
    C. Resource management
    D. Naming service

List the required classes/interfaces that must be provided for an EJB

4. *If you are implementing an entity bean, which class is not required?*
    A. `javax.ejb.EJBObject`
    B. `javax.ejb.EntityBean`
    C. `javax.ejb.EJBRemote`
    D. `java.ejb.EJBHome`

Objective: Distinguish between session and entity beans

5. *Which statement is true about session beans, but is NOT true about entity beans?*
    A. The bean is used as the model in an MVC design pattern.
    B. State is persistent and can represent a row in a database table.
    C. The bean can use a data access object to facilitate migration to CMP.
    D. State represents a conversational state for a specific client.

OBJECTIVE: DISTINGUISH BETWEEN STATEFUL AND STATELESS SESSION BEANS

6. *Which statement is true about stateful session beans, but is NOT true about stateless session beans?*
    A. State can be cached but is not representative of the client state.
    B. State can be cached but is representative of the client state.
    C. State is persistent.
    D. State is cached first, then persisted.

OBJECTIVE: RECOGNIZE APPROPRIATE USES FOR ENTITY, STATEFUL SESSION, AND STATELESS SESSION BEANS

7. *If you have code that deals with workflow of the system and you want the lightest weight EJB, which EJB should you use?*
    A. Entity
    B. Stateful session bean
    C. Stateless session bean
    D. Servlet

OBJECTIVE: EXPLAIN HOW THE EJB CONTAINER DOES LIFE-CYCLE MANAGEMENT AND HAS THE CAPABILITY TO INCREASE SCALABILITY

8. *Which statement about the life cycle of a session bean is true?*
    A. The data in a stateful session bean survives a server's crash
    B. A server that has crashed and been restarted can deserialize cached data for a stateful session bean
    C. A session bean instance can be recreated through the use of a handle.
    D. The container can passivate a stateless session bean to free resources

OBJECTIVE: STATE THE BENEFITS OF BEAN POOLING IN AN EJB CONTAINER

9. *Which statement about bean pooling is true?*
    A. Pooled stateless beans limit interoperability with other server vendors
    B. Pooled entity beans provide connection pooling to the database
    C. Pooling reduces the number of component instances needed
    D. Pooled entity beans provide better support for SQL

OBJECTIVE: STATE THE BENEFITS OF PASSIVATION IN AN EJB CONTAINER.

10. *Which statement on passivation is true?*
   A. Containers must set the transient values to null or zero.
   B. Containers must use Java technology serialization to passivate a bean instance.
   C. Container calls `ejbPassivate` to save the entity bean instance's state to the database.
   D. Container can use any serialization technique to passivate a bean instance as long as it follows Java technology serialization rules.

OBJECTIVE: STATE THE TRANSACTIONAL BEHAVIOR IN A GIVEN SCENARIO FOR AN ENTERPRISE BEAN METHOD WITH A SPECIFIED TRANSACTIONAL ATTRIBUTED AS DEFINED IN THE DEPLOYMENT DESCRIPTOR

11. *Which transaction attribute should be set in the deployment descriptor for a method to guarantee that the method is not invoked with a transaction?*
   A. `RequiresNew`
   B. `Supported`
   C. `Never`
   D. `Mandatory`

OBJECTIVE: STATE THE BENEFITS AND COSTS OF CONTAINER MANAGED PERSISTENCE

12. *Which is a benefit of CMP?*
   A. Faster run-time performance
   B. Rapid development
   C. Less flexible when model changes
   D. Slower developement

OBJECTIVE: IDENTIFY COSTS AND BENEFITS OF USING AN INTERMEDIATE DATA-ACCESS OBJECT BETWEEN AN ENTITY BEAN AND THE DATA RESOURCE

13. *Which is a benefit of using DAOs with BMP-based entity beans?*
   A. Less code than a CMP entity bean
   B. Faster data access than CMP
   C. Reduced coupling with entity bean
   D. Easier to code than CMP entity bean

▼ Exercise Solutions

The following provides the answers to the exercises.

OBJECTIVE: SELECT, FROM A LIST, THE APPLICATION ASPECTS THAT ARE SUITED FOR IMPLEMENTATION USING J2EE

1. *The correct answer is B.*
   An applet is a technology and not an application aspect

OBJECTIVE: IDENTIFY SUITABLE J2EE TECHNOLOGIES FOR THE IMPLEMENTATION OF SPECIFIED APPLICATION ASPECTS

2. *The correct answer is A.*
   JMS is the technology used to implement asynchronous messaging within J2EE. RMI, JNDI, and HTTP do not provide for asynchronous messages.

OBJECTIVE: SELECT, FROM A LIST, THOSE APPLICATION ASPECTS THAT ARE SUITED TO IMPLEMENTATION USING EJB

3. *The correct answer is D.*
   Distribution, security, and resource management are application aspects that you would use EJB to implement. Naming service is an application aspect, but you would use JNDI instead of EJB.

OBJECTIVE: LIST THE REQUIRED CLASSES/INTERFACES THAT MUST BE PROVIDED FOR AN EJB

4. *The correct answer is C.*
   There is no `javax.ejb.EJBRemote` *class*

OBJECTIVE: DISTINGUISH BETWEEN SESSION AND ENTITY BEANS

5. *The correct answer is D.*
   The model in MVC is an entity bean. Entity beans persist data as a row in the database table and CMP is used only for entity beans.

OBJECTIVE: DISTINGUISH BETWEEN STATEFUL AND STATELESS SESSION BEANS

6. *The correct answer is B.*
Answer A is true of stateless and not stateful. A stateful bean is cached, but is not persisted, so answers C and D are incorrect.

OBJECTIVE: RECOGNIZE APPROPRIATE USES FOR ENTITY, STATEFUL SESSION, AND STATELESS SESSION BEANS

7. *The correct answer is C.*
A Servlet is not an EJB, so we can eliminate that option. Each of the EJBs could be used for workflow, but the lightest weight EJB is the stateless session bean.

OBJECTIVE: EXPLAIN HOW THE EJB CONTAINER DOES LIFE-CYCLE MANAGEMENT AND HAS THE CAPABILITY TO INCREASE SCALABILITY

8. *The correct answer is C.*
A session bean can be recreated from the handle that is generated by the session bean. Stateless session beans are never passivated and the only bean to survive a server crash is an entity bean.

OBJECTIVE: STATE THE BENEFITS OF BEAN POOLING IN AN EJB CONTAINER

9. *The correct answer is C.*
Bean pooling is used to reduce the number of components needed to service the users, thus reducing resources for the application.

OBJECTIVE: STATE THE BENEFITS OF PASSIVATION IN AN EJB CONTAINER

10. *The correct answer is D.*
Answer A is false because the specification does not mandate that the container set transient values to null or zero. Answer B is false because the container can use the serialization of choice. Answer C is false because ejbPassivate writes the state to the file system and not the database.

Objective: State the Transactional Behavior in a Given Scenario for an Enterprise Bean Method with a Specified Transactional Attributed as Defined in the Deployment Descriptor

11. *The correct answer is C.*
     You might think the answer could be B (Supported), but this means that if the caller has a transaction, it will get passed to the method.

Objective: State the Benefits and Costs of Container Managed Persistence

12. *The correct answer is B.*
     CMP does allow for rapid development of entity beans. CMP does not necessarily provide faster run-time performance over BMP. It might be true that CMP is less flexible when the model changes, but that would not be a benefit.

Objective: Identify Costs and Benefits of Using an Intermediate Data-Access Object Between an Entity Bean and the Data Resource

13. *The correct answer is C.*
     CMP entity beans are easier and require less code and there is no guarantee which will provide faster data access.

Documenting an Architecture

The current industry standard for visual modeling is the Unified Modeling Language (UML). This chapter starts with an overview of the building blocks of UML, continues with a description of the common mechanisms in UML and then finishes with examples of the different types of UML diagrams along with an explanation of how to interpret these diagrams. By the end of this chapter you will know how to draw and interpret UML diagrams.

After completing this chapter, you will be able to meet the following J2EE Architect exam objectives:

- Explain how to draw UML diagrams to define the system architecture.
- Explain how to interpret UML diagrams.

Introduction

As you create an architecture, you must communicate this system architecture to the designers and developers that will build the system. The best way to describe an architecture is to use visual models and narratives. The visual models are contained in two different documents. The first is the System Requirements document, which contains all of the requirements of the system. The requirements are depicted in a use-case diagram, object diagram, sequence or collaboration diagrams, and activity diagrams. In addition, the use cases are also described in narrative form. The second document is the System Architecture document, which contains the models of the system architecture. You use the class diagram, package diagram, component diagram, deployment diagram and the statechart diagram to visually communicate your architecture. In addition to the visual models in the System Architecture document, you should supply narratives that justify your choices and provide additional description for better understanding.

Prerequisite Review

Using models to define the system architecture is not sufficient. You must support the models with narratives and identify and document your requirements using use cases. This chapter does not cover how to write technically or write use cases to document your requirements and architecture.

Discussion

What is a model? A model is a simplification of reality. You build models using UML diagrams to better understand the system you are developing. The models you build will help you:

- Visualize the system as it is or as you want it to be
- Specify the structure or behavior of a system
- Provide a template to guide the construction of the system
- Document the decisions made about the system

To start modeling with the UML, you need to learn the three major elements of the UML: building blocks, rules for combining building blocks, and common mechanisms. Once you have mastered the three elements, you can read and create UML diagrams.

3.1 The Building Blocks of UML

There are three types of building blocks: elements, relationships, and diagrams. Elements are the abstractions that are first-class citizens in a model; relationships tie these elements together; and diagrams group collections of related elements by means of relationships.

Elements

There are four kinds of elements in UML:

- Structural – Used to create the static parts of a model by representing elements that are conceptual or physical
- Behavioral – Allows you to model the behavior of the system.
- Grouping – Allows you to organize the structural and behavioral elements in your model
- Annotational – Explanatory parts of the model

These elements are the basic elements used in creating models.

Structural Elements

There are seven structural elements: class, interface, collaboration, use case, active class, component, and node.

- A class is a set of objects that share the same attributes, operations, relationships, and semantics. The class is represented by a rectangle with three areas. The first area contains the name of the class, the second area contains the attributes of the class and the third contains the operations of the class. Figure 3–1 illustrates a class.

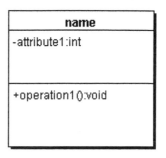

Figure 3–1 *A Class*

- The interface is a collection of operations that specify a service of a class or component. The interface is represented by a rectangle with the same three areas as the class. An interface has the addition of the word "interface" above the interface name to identify it as an interface. Figure 3–2 illustrates an interface.

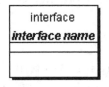

Figure 3–2 *An Interface*

- The collaboration defines an interaction and is a combination of roles and other elements that work together to provide some cooperative behavior that's bigger than the sum of all the elements. The collaboration is represented by a dashed-line ellipse. Figure 3–3 illustrates a collaboration.

Figure 3–3 *A Collaboration*

- A use case is a description of a set of actions that a system performs to yield an observable result of value to an actor. An actor is a person or subsystem outside the bounds of the system to be defined. The visual representation of a use case is the ellipse with the use case name inside the ellipse. Figure 3–4 illustrates a use case.

Figure 3–4 *Use Case*

- The Active class is a class whose objects own one or more processes or threads and therefore can initiate control activity. An active class looks the same as a class with the three areas, but has a bold border. Figure 3–5 illustrates an Active class.

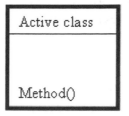

Figure 3–5 *An Active Class*

- A component is a physical and replaceable part of a system that conforms to and provides the realization of a set of interfaces. Visually, the component is a rectangle with two prongs so that it appears that it could be plugged into something. Figure 3–6 illustrates a component.

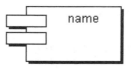

Figure 3–6 *A Component*

- A node is a physical element that exists at run time and represents a computational resource, generally having at least some memory and often processing capability. Visually, the node looks like a cube with a name on the front side of the cube. Figure 3–7 illustrates a node.

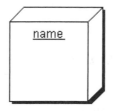

Figure 3–7 *A Node*

Behavioral Elements

Behavioral elements are used to model the behavior of a system. There are two types of behaviors, interaction and state machine. Interaction is a type of behavior element that comprises a set of messages exchanged among a set of objects within a particular context to accomplish a specific purpose. An interaction is represented by a solid arrow line. Figure 3–8 illustrates an arrow.

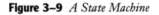

Figure 3–8 *An Arrow*

A state machine is a type of behavior that specifies the sequence of states an object or an interaction goes through during its lifetime in response to events, together with its responses to those events. Figure 3–9 illustrates a state machine.

Figure 3–9 *A State Machine*

Grouping Element

There is only one type of grouping element and that is a package. A package is a general-purpose mechanism for organizing elements into groups. Figure 3–10 illustrates a package.

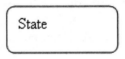

Figure 3–10 *A Package*

Annotational Elements

There is only one type of annotational element and it is a note. A note is a symbol for rendering comments that you want attached to other elements or collections of elements. Visually, the note is represented by a rectangle with the upper right corner folded in. Figure 3–11 illustrates a note.

Figure 3–11 *A Note*

Relationships

There are four standard relationships in UML: dependency, association, generalization, and realization. You use the relationships to create links between the elements in your model.

A dependency is a semantic relationship between two elements in which a change to one thing (the independent thing) can affect the semantics of the other thing (the dependent thing). The dependency is represented as a dashed-line with an arrow on the end. The arrow indicates the direction of the dependency. Using the following diagram, Class1 has a reference to Class2, either passed as a method parameter or defined as a method variable in some method. Figure 3–12 illustrates a dependency relationship.

Figure 3–12 *A Dependency Relationship*

An association is a structural relationship that describes a set of links. A link is a connection among objects. The association is a solid line. Each association has two roles. A role is a direction on the association and can be named with a label.

In the following example, the Company class has a class variable of type Employee and the role of Employee to Company is named Employer. The role of Company to Employee is not named. Each role can have a multiplicity, which is an indication of the number of participants in the relationship. Table 3–1 indicates the different types of multiplicity.

Table 3-1

MULTIPLICITY	MEANING
1	One and only one
0 .. * or *	Zero to infinity
1 ..*	One to infinity
2 .. 4	Range of 2 to 4
2,4	2 or 4

Using the example, a Company has one to many Employees and an Employee can belong to only one Company. Associations also can be navigated (navigability), in the direction of the association and this is represented by an arrow. Navigability indicates whether the object has a responsibility to inform the other object. To put it another way, navigability indicates which object has a class variable referencing the other object. If you have navigability in one direction indicated by an arrow on one end, then you have a unidirectional association. No arrow on either end means you have a bidirectional association. Using the following example, there is no arrow; therefore, the association is bidirectional. This means the Company class has a class variable of type Array, Vector, or Collection that holds objects of type Employee and Employee has a class variable of type Company. Figure 3–13 illustrates an association.

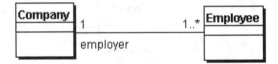

Figure 3–13 *An Association*

Aggregation is a special kind of association, representing a structural relationship between a whole and its parts. The Aggregation association is a diagram with an open diamond on the side of the whole. Using Figure 3–14 , we can see that a Company as the whole is comprised of its parts which is the Employees. Figure 3–14 illustrates an aggregation.

Figure 3–14 *An Aggregation*

Generalization is a specialization/generalization relationship in which objects of the specialized element (child) are substitutable for objects of the generalized element (parent). Generalization is visually represented as a line with a open arrow on the end. The arrow points from the child/subclass to the parent/superclass. Figure 3–15 illustrates a generalization.

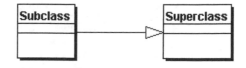

Figure 3–15 *A Generalization*

A realization is a semantic relationship between classifiers, where one classifier specifies a contract that another classifier guarantees to carry out. The realization relationship is represented by a dashed-line with a solid arrow. Figure 3–16 illustrates a realization.

Figure 3–16 *A Realization*

3.2 Common Mechanisms in UML

There are four common mechanisms that apply consistently throughout UML: specifications, adornments, common division, and extensibility.

Specifications

UML is more than just a graphical language. Behind every part of its graphical notation there is a specification that provides a textual statement of the syntax and the semantics of that building block. For example, a class icon has a specification that provides the full set of attributes, operations, and behaviors embodied by that class. Visually, a class icon might show only a small part of the specification or it might show the entire class specification. With this in mind, you could create diagrams with only icons and build up the specification, or you could create the specification by reverse engineering and then build up the diagrams. Figure 3–17 contains the `-attribute1:int` and `+operation1():void`, which are the specification of the class name.

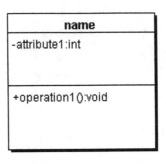

Figure 3–17 *An Example of a Specification of a Class Name*

Adornments

The adornments mechanism indicates whether an element is public, private, or protected respectively represented by +, -, #. In the previous example, `attribute1` is private and `operation1` is public.

Common Divisions

The common division mechanism designates instances of an element. For example, if the element name is underlined, then it is an instance of an element. You can proceed an element name with a : and have an anonymous instance. You can place a name in front of the : and have a named instance of an element. Figure 3–18 contains the `:name`, which means that you have an anonymous instance of class name.

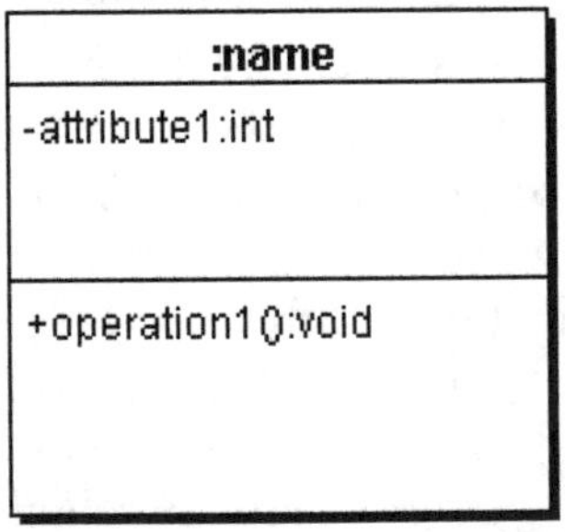

```
            :name
-attribute1:int


+operation1():void


```

Figure 3–18 *Common Division*

Extensibility Mechanisms

Extensibility mechanisms allow you to shape and grow UML to meet your project's requirements. In addition, these mechanisms enable UML to adapt quickly to new technologies by creating new building blocks from the existing UML building blocks.

- Stereotypes – Extends the vocabulary of UML allowing you to create new kinds of building blocks. These building blocks are derived from existing building blocks but are specific to your problem.
- Tagged values – Extends the properties of a UML building block allowing you to create new information in that element's specification.
- Constraints – Extends the semantics of a UML building block, allowing you to add new rules or modify existing ones.

The UML Diagrams

A diagram is the graphical presentation of a set of elements, most often rendered as a connected graph of vertices (elements) and arcs (relationships).

Use-Case Diagram

A use-case diagram shows a set of use cases and actors and their relationships. Use-case diagrams address the static use-case view of a system. These diagrams are especially important in organizing and modeling the behaviors of a system.

Figure 3–19 has actors Customer, Catalog System, Service Rep, and Warehouse. The Customer and Service Rep actors interact with the use-cases Browse Catalog, Search for Product, Create Customer Account, and Checkout. The Browse Catalog and Search for Product use cases retrieve or send information to the Catalog System actor. The Checkout use case retrieves or sends information to the Warehouse actor.

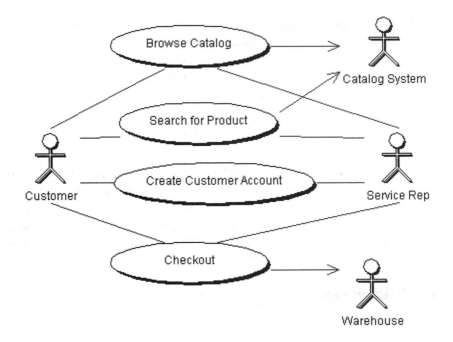

Figure 3–19 *Use-Case Diagram*

Class Diagram

A class diagram shows a set of classes, interfaces, and collaborations and their relationships. These diagrams are the most common diagram found in modeling object-oriented systems. Class diagrams address the static design view of a system. Class diagrams that include active classes address the static process view of a system.

Figure 3–20 shows nine classes. Two of the classes, Buy and Sell, are subclasses of the superlcass Transaction. This diagram tells us that a Customer can have one Cash Account and many Portfolios. A Portfolio has many Accounts, an Account has many Holdings and a Holding has one Stock and can be accessed by many Transactions. The Holding does not know which Transactions are associated to it, because of the navigability. Each Transaction can have only one Holding and one Cash Account. The Transaction can be of type Buy or Sell.

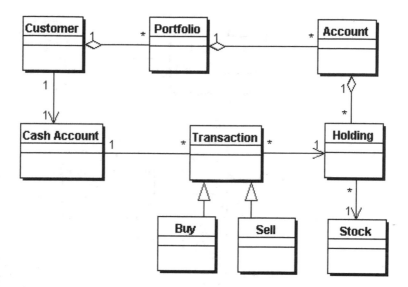

Figure 3–20 *Class Diagram*

Package Diagram

A package diagram is really a special kind of class diagram. Package diagrams represent the organization of the system in groups.

Figure 3–21 uses the stereotype <<subsystem>> to define the Package to be a subsystem. This Package diagram is really a subsystem diagram that shows the subsystems of the system and the dependencies between the subsystems. For example, the CustomerProfile subsystem needs the Security subsystem and is used by the OrderEntry and Marketing subsystems.

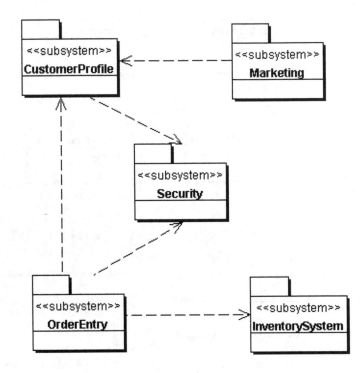

Figure 3–21 *A Package Diagram*

Interaction Diagrams

Both sequence and collaboration diagrams are kinds of interaction diagrams. An interaction diagram shows an interaction, consisting of a set of objects and their relationships, including the messages that can be dispatched among them. Interaction diagrams address the dynamic view of a system. A sequence diagram is an interaction diagram that emphasizes the time-ordering of messages; a collaboration diagram is an interaction diagram that emphasizes the structural organization of the objects that send and receive messages. Sequence and collaboration diagrams are isomorphic, meaning that you can take one and transform it into the other.

All interaction diagrams start with an actor. Figure 3–22 and Figure 3–23 shows the Actor sending a start message to the Start Object, which sends a Create to Object1, which sends a Create to Object2. Object2 sends a loadData message to itself, which is a recursive message. Object2 then returns to Object1 which returns to Start Object. There are no return arrows as returns in interaction diagrams are implicit. The two diagrams are modeling the same flow of events. To understand the flow of events on a collaboration diagram, the messages are numbered making it easier to follow.

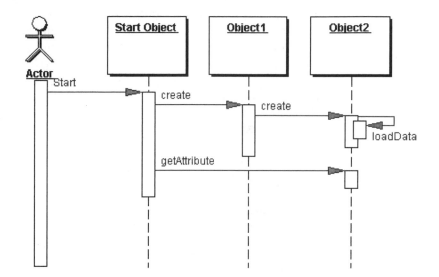

Figure 3–22 *Sequence Diagram*

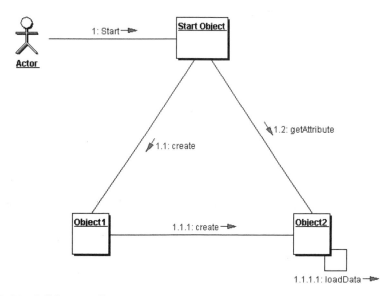

Figure 3–23 *Collaboration Diagram*

Statechart Diagram

A statechart diagram shows a state machine consisting of states, transitions, events, and activities. Statechart diagrams address the dynamic view of a system. They are important in modeling the behavior of an interface, class, or collaboration, and emphasize the event-ordered behavior of an object, which is useful in modeling reactive systems.

Figure 3–24 represents the state of a reservation. Initially, the reservation is on hold and proceeds to a booking state. If successful, then the state of the reservation is booked, if the booking fails then the reservation is cancelled.

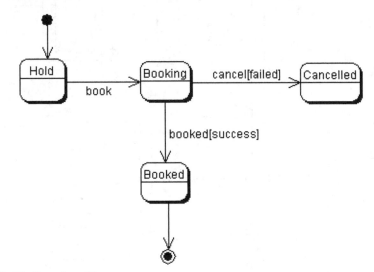

Figure 3–24 *Statechart Diagram*

Activity Diagram

An activity diagram is a special kind of a statechart diagram that shows the flow from activity to activity within a system. An activity diagram addresses the dynamic view of a system. This type of diagram is important in modeling the function of a system and emphasizing the flow of control among objects.

Figure 3–25 starts with Activity1 and then creates parallel execution to Activity2 and Activity3. Activity2 has a two possible outcomes. If Activity2 fails, then proceed to Activity4 and exit. If Activity2 succeeds, then proceed to Activity5 and join with the parallel execution from Activity3. After Activity3 and Activity5 are joined, execution continues with Activity6 and then completes.

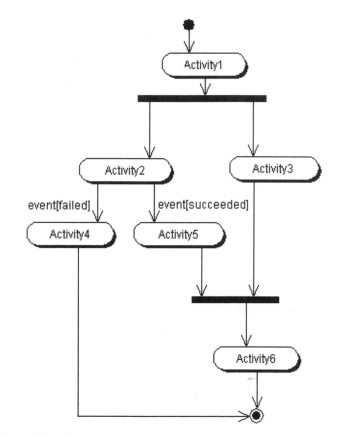

Figure 3–25 *Activity Diagram*

Component Diagram

A component diagram shows the organizations and dependencies among a set of components. Component diagrams address the static implementation view of a system. They are related to class diagrams in that a component diagram typically maps to one or more classes, interfaces, or collaborations.

Figure 3–26 uses stereotypes to create new J2EE-specific components of JSP, Servlet, and SessionBean. The Search component sends requests to the SearchController component, which makes a request to the SearchEngine and sends the results to the SearchResults JSP. The SearchEngine component uses the ICatalog interface to retrieve information from the Catalog subsystem.

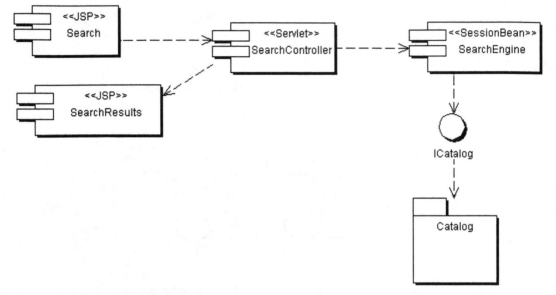

Figure 3–26 *Component Diagram*

Deployment Diagram

A deployment diagram shows the configuration of run-time processing nodes and the components that live on these nodes. Deployment diagrams address the static deployment view of an architecture. They are related to component diagrams in that a node typically encloses one or more components.

Figure 3–27 shows a four node system configuration. The Browser uses HTTP to communicate with the Web server, which runs the SearchController servlet, Search JSP, and SearchResults JSP. The Web server uses RMI to communicate with the Application server, which runs the Search Engine sessionbean. The Application Server uses IIOP to communicate with the Catalog System node.

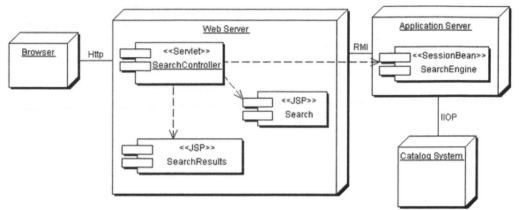

Figure 3–27 *Deployment Diagram*

Essential Points

The following summarizes the most important points described in this chapter:

- UML has three kinds of building blocks: elements, relationships, and diagrams.
- There are four kinds of elements, which are the basic elements used to create UML:

    Structural elements create the static parts of a model by representing conceptual or physical elements.

    Behavioral elements allow you to model the behavior of the system.

    Grouping elements allow you to organize the structural and behavioral elements in a model.

    Annotational elements describe the parts of the model

- Relationships create links between the elements in your model. There are four standard relationships in UML:

    Dependency – A semantic relationship between two elements in which a change to one thing (the independent thing) can affect the semantics of the other thing (the dependent thing).

    Associate – A structural relationship that describes a set of links.

    Generalization – A specialization/generalization relationship in which you can substitute objects of the specialized element (child) for objects of the generalized element (parent).

Realization – A semantic relationship between classifiers, where one classifier specifies a contract that another classifier guarantees to carry out.

- There are four common mechanisms in UML:

Specifications – A textual statement of the syntax and the semantics of that building block.

Adornments – A symbol to indicate whether an element is public, private, or protected

Common division – A symbol to designate instances of an element.

Extensibility – A method to shape and grow UML to meet your project's requirements. There are three types of extensibility mechanisms:

Stereotypes – Extends the vocabulary of a UML building block.

Tagged values – Extends the properties of a UML building block.

Constraints – Extends the semantics of a UML building block.

- A diagram is the graphical presentation of a set of elements.

A use-case diagram shows a set of use cases and the actors and their relationships.

A class diagram shows a set of classes, interfaces, and collaborations and their relationships.

A package diagram is a special kind of class diagram that organizes the system into groups.

An interaction diagram shows an interaction, consisting of a set of objects and their relationships.

Statechart diagram describes the dynamic view of a system.

An activity diagram is a statechart diagram that shows the flow from activity to activity within the system.

A component diagram shows the organizations and dependencies among a set of components.

A deployment diagram shows the configuration of run-time processing nodes and the components on these nodes.

▼ Review Your Progress

This section reviews the objectives described in the chapter and provides review questions to ensure that you understand the important points in the chapter.

OBJECTIVE: DRAWING UML DIAGRAMS TO EXPLAIN THE SYSTEM ARCHITECTURE

1. *Which type of diagram is displayed?*

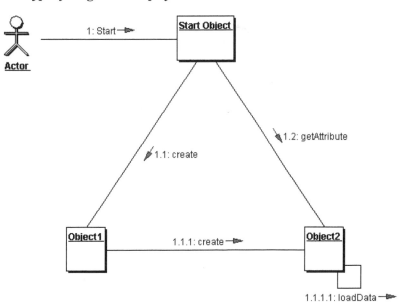

A. Class diagram

B. Deployment diagram

C. Component diagram

D. Package diagram

2. *Which type of diagram is displayed?*

    A. Activity diagram

    B. Class diagram

    C. Collaboration diagram

    D. Sequence diagram

    E. State diagram

OBJECTIVE: EXPLAIN HOW TO INTERPRET UML DIAGRAMS

3. Which statement is true about the diagram?

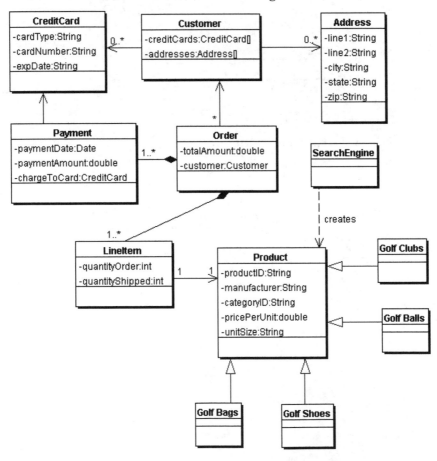

    A. CreditCard holds a reference to Customer

    B. Customer holds a reference to Address

    C. LineItem holds a reference to Order

    D. CreditCard holds a reference to Payment

4. *What is true about the diagram?*

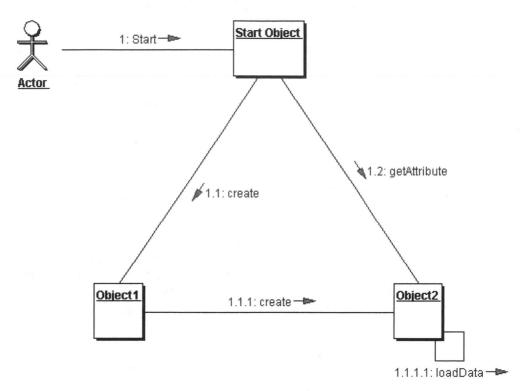

A. The StartObject class issues a create to Object2

B. The class Object1 issues a loadData on Object2

C. The class Object2 calls the getAttribute method

D. The object method loadData is self-called

▼ Exercise Solutions

The following provides the answers to the exercises.

OBJECTIVE: DRAWING UML DIAGRAMS TO EXPLAIN THE SYSTEM ARCHITECTURE

1. *The correct answer is B.*
This is a deployment diagram that shows the nodes of a system and how the nodes communicate. Yes, it does show components and you might think it is a

component diagram, but the components are part of the nodes, which is the distinguishing feature of a deployment diagram.

2.   *The correct answer is C.*
This is a collaboration diagram that shows messages sent between objects in the system. It is not a class diagram, because a class diagram does not show messages between the objects. It is not an activity diagram, because the activity diagram uses elipses for the activities. The state diagram looks similar, but the state diagram shows the state of the same object instead of having multiple objects, such as in this diagram.

OBJECTIVE: INTERPRETING UML DIAGRAMS

3.   *The correct answer is B.*
The Customer holds a reference to an Address, which is depicted by the arrow point from Customer to Address. Answer A is wrong because the arrow is pointing towards CreditCard instead of pointing to Customer. Answer D is wrong for the same reason, the navigability is pointing in the wrong direction. Answer C is wrong because the Order is comprised of LineItems.

4.   *The correct answer is D.*
Object2 is doing a recursive call to itself. Answer A is incorrect because Start-Object is sending a create to Object1 instead of Object2. Answer B is incorrect because it is StartObject calling Object2 instead of the other way around. Answer C is incorrect because Object1 calls Object2 with a create and not a loadData.

Design Patterns

 Creational Patterns

 Structural Patterns

 Behavorial Patterns

Patterns were first used by a building architect named Christopher Alexander in the 1970s. He realized that there were certain solutions that you could apply over and over again to the same or similar problems. He also combined these existing solutions to create new solutions to a new problem. In 1987, Ward Cunningham and Kent Beck developed five patterns to use in interface design. But it wasn't until 1994 that Erich Gamma, Richard Helm, John Vlissides, and Ralph Johnson published the now famous book *Design Patterns: Elements of Reusable Object-Oriented Software*, which described a way of documenting patterns that has become the industry standard. These men are often referred to as the Gang of Four (GoF). As new patterns are developed, most follow the documentation standards described by the Design Patterns book.

This chapter describes how you can use patterns to help you create an architecture. These patterns are usually at the object and class level, but they can also be abstracted to a higher level.

After completing this chapter, you will be able to meet the following J2EE technology architect exam objectives:

- From a list, select the most appropriate design pattern for a given scenario. Patterns will be limited to those documented in Gamma et al. and named using the names given in that book.
- State the benefits of using design patterns.
- State the name of a Gamma et al. design pattern given the UML diagram and/or a brief description of the patterns's functionality.
- From a list, select the benefits of a specified Gamma et al. design pattern.
- Identify the Gamma et al. design pattern associated with a specified J2EE feature.

Prerequisite Review

This chapter assumes that you are already familiar with the Gang of Four (GoF) patterns, as described in *"Design Patterns: Elements of Reusable Object-Oriented Software."* This chapter reviews the patterns in the context of the exam objectives to cover the material necessary for the exam.

Discussion

A design pattern is a common solution to a common problem encountered in software development. In this chapter, we have described the patterns in terms of the following:

- Name – A label used to identify the problem, solution, and consequences of a pattern. The pattern name should be descriptive and kept to one or two words.
- Description – A short description of the pattern, a UML diagram, and code sample are all used to help define the pattern.
- Benefits – Describes the advantages using the specified pattern.
- When to Use – Describes when in the application design you should use the pattern.

There are three types of the GoF patterns:

- Creational
- Structural
- Behavioral

4.1 Creational Patterns

Creational patterns support the creation of objects in a system. Creational patterns allow objects to be created in a system without having to identify a specific class type in the code, so you do not have to write large, complex code to instantiate an object. It does this by having the subclass of the class create the objects. However, this can limit the type or number of objects that can be created within a system.

The following Creational patterns are described:

- Abstract Factory
- Builder
- Factory Method
- Prototype
- Singleton

Abstract Factory Pattern

This pattern provides an interface for creating families of related or dependent objects without specifying their concrete classes.

Given a set of related abstract classes, the Abstract Factory pattern provides a way to create instances of those abstract classes from a matched set of concrete subclasses. Figure 4–1 illustrates the Abstract Factory pattern.

The Abstract Factory pattern provides an abstract class that determines the appropriate concrete class to instantiate to create a set of concrete products that implement a standard interface. The client interacts only with the product interfaces and the Abstract Factory class. The client never knows about the concrete construction classes, provided by this pattern.

The Abstract Factory pattern is similar to the Factory Method pattern, except it creates families of related objects.

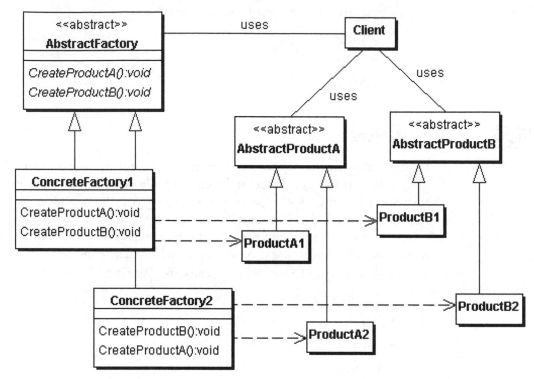

Figure 4–1 *The Abstract Factory Pattern*

BENEFITS

The following lists the benefits of using the Abstract Factory pattern:

- Isolates concrete classes.
- Makes exchanging product families easy.
- Promotes consistency among products.

WHEN TO USE

You should use the Abstract Factory pattern when:

- The system should be independent of how its products are created, composed, and represented.
- The system should be configured with one of multiple families of products, for example, Microsoft Windows or Apple McIntosh classes.
- The family of related product objects is designed to be used together, and you must enforce this constraint. This is the key point of the pattern, otherwise you could use a Factory Method.

- You want to provide a class library of products, and reveal only their interfaces, not their implementations.

Builder Pattern

The Builder pattern separates the construction of a complex object from its representation so the same construction process can create different objects. The Builder pattern allows a client object to construct a complex object by specifying only its type and content. The client is shielded from the details of the object's construction. This simplifies the creation of complex objects by defining a class that builds instances of another class. The Builder pattern produces one main product and there might be more than one class in the product, but there is always one main class. Figure 4–2 illustrates the Builder pattern. When you use the Builder pattern, you create the complex objects one step at a time. Other patterns build the object in a single step.

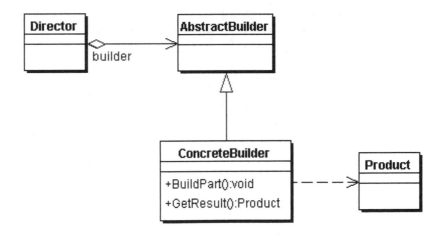

Figure 4–2 *The Builder Pattern*

BENEFITS

The following lists the benefits of using the Builder pattern:

- Lets you vary a product's internal representation.
- Isolates code for construction and representation.
- Gives you greater control over the construction process.

WHEN TO USE

You should use the Builder pattern when:

- The algorithm for creating a complex object should be independent of both the parts that make up the object and how these parts are assembled.
- The construction process must allow different representations of the constructed object.

Factory Method Pattern

The Factory Method pattern defines an interface for creating an object, but lets the subclasses decide which class to instantiate. The Factory method lets a class defer instantiation to subclasses, which is useful for constructing individual objects for a specific purpose without the requestor knowing the specific class being instantiated. This allows you to introduce new classes without modifying the code because the new class implements only the interface so it can be used by the client. You create a new factory class to create the new class and the factory class implements the factory interface. Figure 4–3 illustrates the Factory Method pattern.

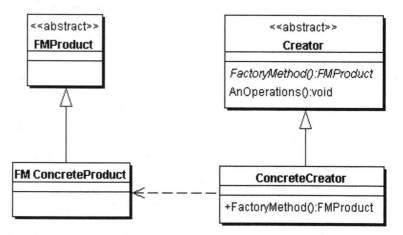

Figure 4–3 *The Factory Method Pattern*

BENEFITS

The following lists the benefits of using the Factory Method pattern:

- Eliminates the need to bind application classes into your code. The code deals only with the interface, so you can work with any classes that implement that interface.

- Enables the subclasses to provide an extended version of an object, because creating an object inside a class is more flexible than creating the object directly in the client.

WHEN TO USE

You should use the Factory Method pattern when:

- A class cannot anticipate the class of objects it must create.
- A class wants its subclasses to specify the objects it creates.
- Classes delegate responsibility to one of several helper subclasses, and you want to localize the knowledge of which helper subclass is the delegate.

Prototype Pattern

The Prototype pattern allows an object to create customized objects without knowing their exact class or the details of how to create them. It specifies the kinds of objects to create using a prototypical instance, and creates new objects by copying this prototype. The Prototype pattern works by giving prototypical objects to an object and then initiates the creation of objects. The creation-initiating object then creates objects by asking the prototypical objects to make copies of themselves. The Prototype pattern makes creating objects dynamically easier by defining classes whose objects can duplicate themselves. Figure 4–4 illustrates the Prototype pattern.

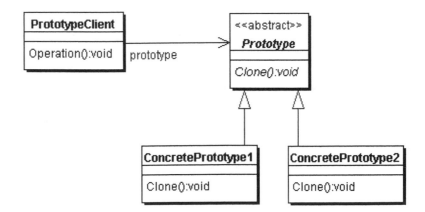

Figure 4–4 *The Prototype Pattern*

BENEFITS

The following lists the benefits of using the Prototype pattern:

- Adding and removing products at run time
- Specifying new objects by varying values
- Specifying new objects by varying structure
- Reduced subclassing
- Configuring an application with classes dynamically

WHEN TO USE

You should use the Prototype pattern when:

- The classes to instantiate are specified at run time, for example, by dynamic loading.
- To avoid building a class hierarchy of factories that parallels the class hierarchy of products.
- When instances of a class can have one of only a few different combinations of state.

Singleton Pattern

The Singleton pattern ensures that a class has only one instance, and provides a global point of access to that class. It ensures that all objects that use an instance of this class use the same instance. Figure 4–5 illustrates the Singleton pattern.

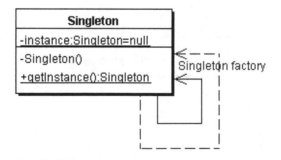

Figure 4–5 *The Singleton Pattern*

BENEFITS

The following lists the benefits of using the Singleton pattern:

- Controlled access to sole instance
- Reduced name space
- Permits refinement of operations and representation
- Permits a variable number of instances
- More flexible than class operations

WHEN TO USE

You should use the Singleton pattern when:

- There must be exactly one instance of a class.

4.2 Structural Patterns

Structural patterns control the relationships between large portions of your applications. Structural patterns affect applications in a variety of ways, for example, the Adapter pattern enables two incompatible systems to communicate, while the Façade pattern enables you to present a simplified inter-face to a user without removing all the options available in the system.

Structural patterns allow you to create systems without rewriting or customizing the code. This provides the system with enhanced reusability and robust functionality.

The following Structural patterns are described:

- Adapter
- Bridge
- Composite
- Decorator
- Façade
- Flyweight
- Proxy

Adapter Pattern

The Adapter pattern acts as an intermediary between two classes, converting the interface of one class so that it can be used with the other. This enables classes with incompatible interfaces to work together. The Adapter pattern implements an interface known to its clients and provides access to an instance of a class not known to its clients. An adapter object provides the functionality of an interface without having to know the class used to implement that interface. Figure 4–6 illustrates the Adapter pattern.

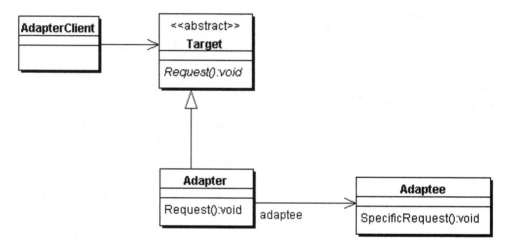

Figure 4–6 *The Adapter Pattern*

BENEFITS

The following lists the benefits of using the Adapter pattern:

- Allows two or more incompatible objects to communicate and interact
- Improves reusability of older functionality

WHEN TO USE

You should use the Adapter pattern when:

- You want to use an existing class, and its interface does not match the interface you need.

- You want to create a reusable class that cooperates with unrelated or unforeseen classes, that is, classes that don't necessarily have compatible interfaces.
- You want to use an object in an environment that expects an interface that is different from the object's interface.
- Interface translation among multiple sources must occur.

Bridge Pattern

The Bridge pattern divides a complex component into two separate but related inheritance hierarchies: the functional abstraction and the internal implementation. This makes it easier to change either aspect of the component so that the two can vary independently.

The Bridge pattern is useful when there is a hierarchy of abstractions and a corresponding hierarchy of implementations. Rather than combining the abstractions and implementations into many distinct classes, the Bridge pattern implements the abstractions and implementations as independent classes that can be combined dynamically. Figure 4–7 illustrates the Bridge pattern.

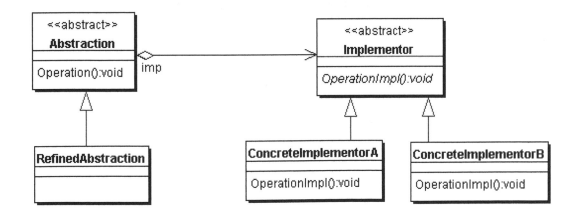

Figure 4–7 *The Bridge Pattern*

BENEFITS

The following lists the benefits of using the Bridge pattern:

- Enables you to separate the interface from the implementation
- Improves extensibility
- Hides implementation details from clients

WHEN TO USE

You should use the Bridge pattern when:

- You want to avoid a permanent binding between an abstraction and its implementation.
- Both the abstractions and their implementations should be extensible using subclasses.
- Changes in the implementation of an abstraction should have no impact on clients; that is, you should not have to recompile their code.

Composite Pattern

The Composite pattern enables you to create hierarchical tree structures of varying complexity, while allowing every element in the structure to operate with a uniform interface. The Composite pattern combines objects into tree structures to represent either the whole hierarchy or a part of the hierarchy. This means the Composite pattern allows clients to treat individual objects and compositions of objects uniformly. Figure 4–8 illustrates the Composite pattern.

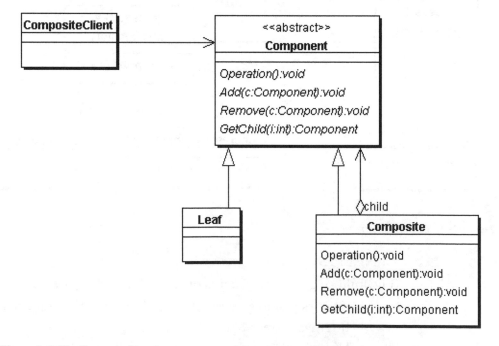

Figure 4–8 *The Composite Pattern*

BENEFITS

The following lists the benefits of using the Composite pattern:

- Defines class hierarchies consisting of primitive objects and composite objects
- Makes it easier to add new kinds of components
- Provides flexibility of structure and a manageable interface

WHEN TO USE

You should use the Composite pattern when:

- You want to represent the whole hierarchy or a part of the hierarchy of objects.
- You want clients to be able to ignore the difference between compositions of objects and individual objects.
- The structure can have any level of complexity, and is dynamic.

Decorator Pattern

The Decorator pattern enables you to add or remove object functionality without changing the external appearance or function of the object. It changes the functionality of an object in a way that is transparent to its clients by using an instance of a subclass of the original class that delegates operations to the original object. The Decorator pattern attaches additional responsibilities to an object dynamically to provide a flexible alternative to changing object functionality without using static inheritance. Figure 4–9 illustrates the Decorator pattern.

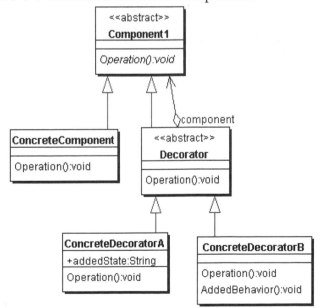

Figure 4–9 *The Decorator Pattern*

BENEFITS

The following lists the benefits of using the Decorator pattern:

- More flexibility than static inheritance
- Avoids feature-laden classes high up in the hierarchy
- Simplifies coding because you write a series of classes, each targeted at a specific part of the functionality, rather than coding all behavior into the object
- Enhances the object's extensibility because you make changes by coding new classes

WHEN TO USE

You should use the Decorator pattern when:

- You want to add responsibilities to individual objects dynamically and transparently, that is, without affecting other objects.
- You want to add responsibilities to the object that you might want to change in the future.
- When extension by static subclassing is impractical.

Façade Pattern

The Façade pattern provides a unified interface to a group of interfaces in a subsystem. The Façade pattern defines a higher-level interface that makes the subsystem easier to use because you have only one interface. This unified interface enables an object to access the subsystem using the interface to communicate with the subsystem. Figure 4–10 illustrates the Façade pattern.

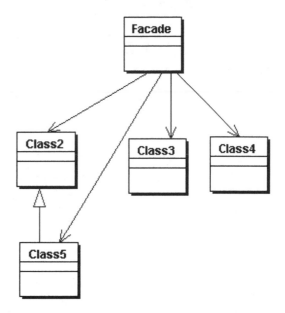

Figure 4–10 *The Façade Pattern*

BENEFITS

The following lists the benefits of using the Façade pattern:

- Provides a simple interface to a complex system without reducing the options provided by the system.
- Shields clients from subsystem components.
- Promotes weak coupling between the subsystem and its clients.
- Reduces coupling between subsystems if every subsystem uses its own Façade pattern and other parts of the system use the Façade pattern to communicate with the subsystem.
- Translates the client requests to the subsystems that can fulfill those requests.

WHEN TO USE

You should use the Façade pattern when:

- You want to provide a simple interface to a complex subsystem.
- There are many dependencies between clients and the implementation classes of an abstraction.
- You want to layer your subsystems.

Flyweight Pattern

The Flyweight pattern reduces the number of low-level, detailed objects within a system by sharing objects. If instances of a class that contain the same information can be used interchangeably, the Flyweight pattern allows a program to avoid the expense of multiple instances that contain the same information by sharing one instance. Figure 4–11 illustrates the Flyweight pattern.

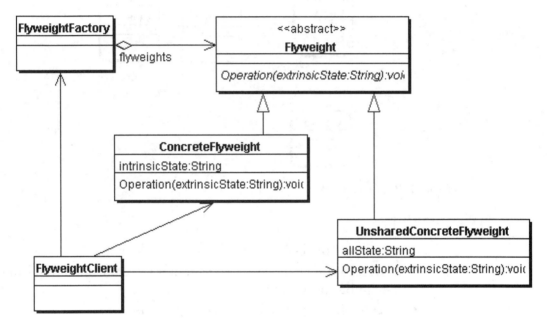

Figure 4–11 *The Flyweight Pattern*

BENEFITS

The following lists the benefits of using the Flyweight pattern:

- Reduction in the number of objects to handle
- Reduction in memory and on storage devices, if the objects are persisted

WHEN TO USE

You should use the Flyweight pattern when all of the following are true:

- The application uses a large number of objects.
- Storage costs are high because of the quantity of objects.
- The application doesn't depend on object identity.

Proxy Pattern

The Proxy pattern provides a surrogate or placeholder object to control access to the original object. There are several types of implementations of the Proxy pattern with the Remote proxy and Virtual proxy being the most common. Figure 4–12 illustrates the Proxy pattern.

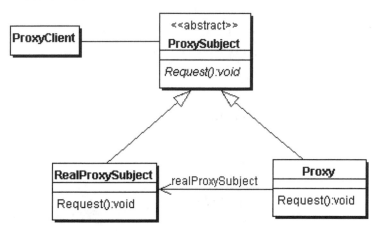

Figure 4–12 *The Proxy Pattern*

BENEFITS

The following lists the benefits of using the Proxy pattern:

- A remote proxy can hide the fact that an object resides in a different address space.
- A virtual proxy can perform optimizations, such as creating an object on demand.

WHEN TO USE

You should use the Proxy pattern when:

- You need a more versatile or sophisticated reference to an object than a simple pointer.

4.3 Behavioral Patterns

Behavioral patterns influence how state and behavior flow through a system. By optimizing how state and behavior are transferred and modified, you can simplify, optimize, and increase the maintainability of an application.

The following Behavioral patterns are described:

- Chain of Responsibility
- Command
- Interpreter
- Iterator
- Mediator
- Memento
- Observer
- State
- Strategy
- Template Method
- Visitor

Chain of Responsibility Pattern

The Chain of Responsibility pattern establishes a chain within a system, so that a message can either be handled at the level where it is first received, or be directed to an object that can handle it. Figure 4–13 illustrates the Chain of Responsibility pattern.

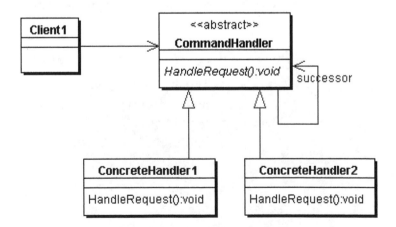

Figure 4–13 *The Chain of Responsibility Pattern*

BENEFITS

The following lists the benefits of using the Chain of Responsibility pattern:

- Reduced coupling
- Added flexibility in assigning responsibilities to objects
- Allows a set of classes to behave as a whole, because events produced in one class can be sent on to other handler classes within the composite

WHEN TO USE

You should use the Chain of Responsibility pattern when:

- More than one object can handle a request, and the handler isn't known.
- You want to issue a request to one of several objects without specifying the receiver explicitly.
- The set of objects that can handle a request should be specified dynamically.

Command Pattern

The Command pattern encapsulates a request in an object, which enables you to store the command, pass the command to a method, and return the command like any other object. Figure 4–14 illustrates the Command pattern.

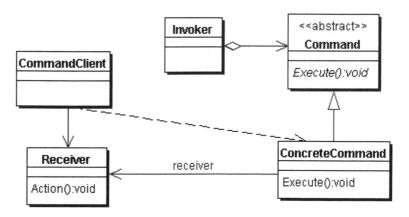

Figure 4–14 *The Command Pattern*

BENEFITS

The following lists the benefits of using the Command pattern:

- Separates the object that invokes the operation from the one that knows how to perform it.
- It's easy to add new commands, because you don't have to change existing classes.

WHEN TO USE

You should use the Command pattern when:

- You want to parameterize objects by an action to perform.
- You specify, queue, and execute requests at different times.
- You must support undo, logging, or transactions.

Interpreter Pattern

The Interpreter pattern interprets a language to define a representation for its grammar along with an interpreter that uses the representation to interpret sentences in the language. Figure 4–15 illustrates the Interpreter pattern.

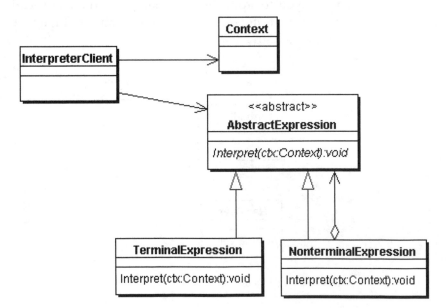

Figure 4–15 *The Interpreter Pattern*

BENEFITS

The following lists the benefits of using the Interpreter pattern:
- Easy to change and extend the grammar
- Implementing the grammar is easy

WHEN TO USE

You should use the Interpreter pattern when:
- The grammar of the language is simple.
- Efficiency is not a critical concern.

Iterator Pattern

The Iterator pattern provides a consistent way to sequentially access items in a collection that is independent of and separate from the underlying collection. Figure 4–16 illustrates the Iterator pattern.

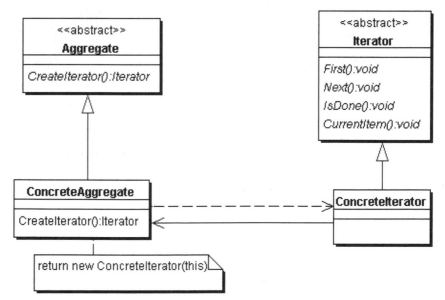

Figure 4–16 *The Iterator Pattern*

BENEFITS

The following lists the benefits of using the Iterator pattern:
- Supports variations in the traversal of a collection
- Simplifies the interface of the collection

When to Use

You should use the Iterator pattern when you want to:

- Access collection object's contents without exposing its internal representation.
- Support multiple traversals of objects in a collection.
- Provide a uniform interface for traversing different structures in a collection.

Mediator Pattern

The Mediator pattern simplifies communication among objects in a system by introducing a single object that manages message distribution among other objects. The Mediator pattern promotes loose coupling by keeping objects from referring to each other explicitly, and it lets you vary their interaction independently. Figure 4–17 illustrates the Mediator pattern.

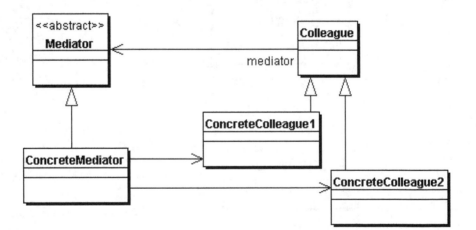

Figure 4–17 *The Mediator Pattern*

BENEFITS

The following lists the benefits of using the Mediator pattern:

- Decouples colleagues
- Simplifies object protocols
- Centralizes control

- The individual components become simpler and easier to deal with, because they no longer need to directly pass messages to each other
- Components are more generic, because they no longer need to contain logic to deal with their communication with other components.

WHEN TO USE

You should use the Mediator pattern when:

- A set of objects communicate in well-defined but complex ways.
- You want to customize a behavior that's distributed between several objects without using subclasses.

Memento Pattern

The Memento pattern preserves a "snapshot" of an object's state, so that the object can return to its original state without having to reveal its content to the rest of the world. Figure 4–18 illustrates the Memento pattern.

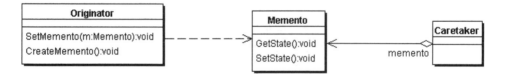

Figure 4–18 *The Memento Pattern*

BENEFITS

The following lists the benefits of using the Memento pattern:

- Preserves encapsulation boundaries
- Simplifies the originator

WHEN TO USE

You should use the Memento pattern when:

- A snapshot of an object's state must be saved so that it can be restored to that state later.
- Using a direct interface to obtain the state would expose implementation details and break the object's encapsulation.

Observer Pattern

The Observer pattern provides a way for a component to flexibly broadcast messages to interested receivers. It defines a one-to-many dependency between objects so that when one object changes state, all its dependents are notified and updated automatically. Figure 4–19 illustrates the Observer pattern.

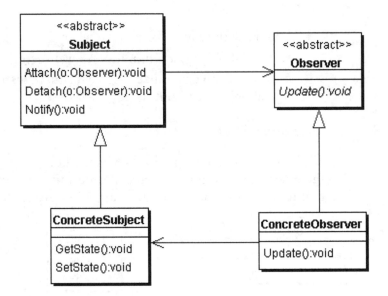

Figure 4–19 *The Observer Pattern*

BENEFITS

The following lists the benefits of using the Observer pattern:
- Abstract coupling between subject and observer
- Support for broadcast communication

WHEN TO USE

You should use the Observer pattern when:
- A change to one object requires changing the other object and you don't know how many objects need to change.
- An object should be able to notify other objects without making assumptions about the identity of those objects.

State Pattern

The State pattern allows an object to alter its behavior when its internal state changes. The object appears to change its class. Figure 4–20 illustrates the State pattern.

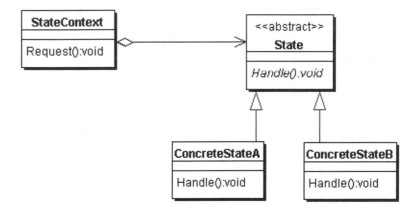

Figure 4–20 *The State Pattern*

BENEFITS

The following lists the benefits of using the State pattern:

- Localizes state-specific behavior and partitions behavior for different states
- Makes state transitions explicit

WHEN TO USE

You should use the State pattern when:

- An object's behavior depends on its state and it must change its behavior at run-time depending on that state.
- Operations have large, multipart conditional statements that depend on the object's state.

Strategy Pattern

The Strategy pattern defines a group of classes that represent a set of possible behaviors. These behaviors can then be used in an application to change its functionality. Figure 4–21 illustrates the Strategy pattern.

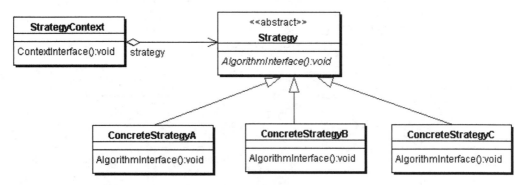

Figure 4–21 *The Strategy Pattern*

BENEFITS

The following lists the benefits of using the Strategy pattern:
- An alternative to subclassing
- Defines each behavior in its own class, which eliminates conditional statements
- Easier to extend a model to incorporate new behaviors without recoding the application.

WHEN TO USE

You should use the Strategy pattern when:
- Many related classes differ only in their behavior.
- You need different variants of an algorithm.
- An algorithm uses data unknown to clients.

Template Method Pattern

The Template Method pattern provides a method that allows subclasses to override parts of the method without rewriting it. Define the skeleton of an algorithm in an operation, deferring some steps to subclasses. Template method lets subclasses redefine certain steps of an algorithm without changing the algorithm's structure. Figure 4–22 illustrates the Template Method pattern.

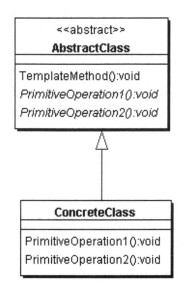

Figure 4–22 *The Template Method Pattern*

BENEFITS

The following lists the benefit of using the Template Method pattern:

- Fundamental technique for reusing code

WHEN TO USE

You should use the Template Method pattern when:

- You want to implement the invariant parts of an algorithm once and use subclasses to implement the behavior that can vary.
- When common behavior among subclasses should be factored and localized in a common class to avoid code duplication.

Visitor Pattern

The Visitor pattern provides a maintainable, easy way to represent an operation to be performed on the elements of an object structure. The Visitor pattern lets you define a new operation without changing the classes of the elements on which it operates. Figure 4–23 illustrates the Visitor pattern.

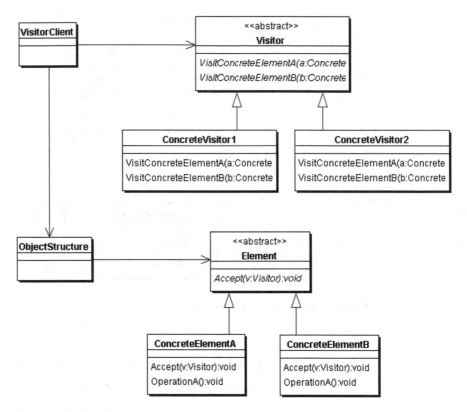

Figure 4–23 *The Visitor Pattern*

BENEFITS

The following lists the benefits of using the Visitor pattern:

- Makes adding new operations easy
- Gathers related operations and separates unrelated ones

WHEN TO USE

You should use the Visitor pattern when:

- An object structure contains many classes of objects with differing interfaces and you want to perform operations on these objects that depend on their concrete classes.
- Classes defining the object structure rarely change but you often want to define new operations over the structure.

Essential Points

The following summarizes the most important points described in this chapter:

- Creational patterns allow objects to be created in a system without having to identify a specific class type in the code, so you do not have to write large, complex code to instantiate an object.
- The Abstract Factory pattern provides an interface for creating families of related or dependent objects without specifying their concrete classes.
- The Builder pattern separates the construction of a complex object from its represenation so the same construction process can create different objects.
- The Factory Method pattern defines an interface for creating an object, but lets the subclasses decide which class to instantiate.
- The Prototype pattern allows an object to create customized objects without knowing their exact class or the details of how to create them.
- The Singleton pattern ensures that a class has only one instance, and provides a global point of access to that class.
- Structural patterns control the relationships between large portions of your applications.
- The Adapter pattern acts as an intermediary between two classes, converting the interface of one class so that it can be used with the other.
- The Bridge pattern divides a complex component into two separate but related inheritance hierarchies: the functional abstraction and the internal implementation.
- The Composite pattern enables you to create hierarchical tree structures of varying complexity, while allowing every element in the structure to operate with a uniform interface.
- The Decorator pattern enables you to add or remove object functionality without changing the external appearance or function of the object.
- The Façade pattern provides a unified interface to a group of interfaces in a subsystem.

- The Flyweight pattern reduces the number of low-level, detailed objects within a system by sharing objects.
- The Proxy pattern provides a surrogate or placeholder object to control access to the original object.
- Behavioral patterns influence how state and behavior flow through a system.
- The Chain of Responsibility pattern establishes a chain within a system, so that a message can either be handled at the level where it is first received, or be directed to an object that can handle it.
- The Command pattern encapsulates a request in an object, which enables you to store the command, pass the command to a method, and return the command like any other object.
- The Interpreter pattern interprets a language to define a representation for its grammar along with an interpreter that uses the representation to interpret sentences in the language.
- The Iterator pattern provides a consistent way to sequentially access items in a collection that is independent of and separate from the underlying collection.
- The Mediator pattern simplifies communication among objects in a system by introducing a single object that manages message distribution among other objects.
- The Memento pattern preserves a "snapshot" of an object's state, so that the object can return to its original state without having to reveal its content to the rest of the world
- The Observer pattern provides a way for a component to flexibly broadcast messages to interested receivers.
- The State pattern allows an object to alter its behavior when its internal state changes.
- The Strategy pattern defines a group of classes that represent a set of possible behaviors.
- The Template Method pattern provides a method that allows subclasses to override parts of the method without rewriting it.
- The Visitor pattern provides a maintainable, easy way to represent an operation to be performed on the elements of an object structure.

▼ Review Your Progress

This section reviews the objectives described in the chapter and provides review questions to ensure that you understand the important points in the chapter.

OBJECTIVE: SELECT THE MOST APPROPRIATE DESIGN PATTERN FOR A GIVEN SCENARIO

1. *Which pattern would you use to create a complex object and have the assembly and parts independent?*
   A. Prototype
   B. Singleton
   C. Builder
   D. Abstract Factory

2. *You are asked to interface with a class in an existing system, but the interface does not match the interface you need. Which pattern would you use?*
   A. Decorator
   B. Abstract Factory
   C. Command
   D. Adapter

OBJECTIVE: STATE THE NAME OF A DESIGN PATTERN, GIVEN THE UML DIAGRAM

3. *Which pattern allows for addition of responsibilities?*
   A. Proxy
   B. Façade
   C. Decorator
   D. Strategy
   E. Adapter

4. *Which pattern is shown in the diagram?*

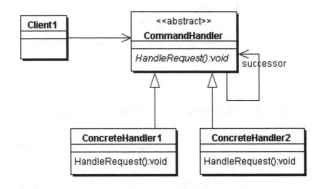

A. Command
B. Observer
C. Chain of Responsibility
D. Composite

OBECTIVE: FROM A LIST, SELECT THE BENEFITS OF A DESIGN PATTERN

5. *What are two benefits of the Facade pattern? (Choose two.)*
   A. It hides complex subsystems from clients.
   B. It allows objects to masquerade as different objects.
   C. It decouples the object interface from the implementation.
   D. It encourages weak coupling between the client and the subsystem.

6. *What are two benefits of the Singleton pattern? (Choose two.)*
   A. It encourages use of global variables.
   B. It controls access to a single instance.
   C. It permits a variable number of instances.
   D. It allows a collection of objects to be manipulated as a single object

OBJECTIVE: IDENTIFY THE DESIGN PATTERN ASSOCIATED WITH A SPECIFIED J2EE FEATURE

7. *Which pattern is used by the Home Interface of an EJB?*
    A. Proxy
    B. Decorator
    C. Mediator
    D. Factory

▼ Exercise Solutions

The following provides the answers to the exercises.

OBJECTIVE: SELECT THE MOST APPROPRIATE DESIGN PATTERN FOR A GIVEN SCENARIO.

1. *The correct answer is C.*
    The Builder patterns allows you to create complex objects and keep the parts and the assembling of those parts separate and independent.

2. *The correct answer is D.*
    The Adapter pattern allows you to adapt the interface of a class or component to meet your needs.

OBJECTIVE: STATE THE NAME OF A DESIGN PATTERN, GIVEN THE UML DIAGRAM.

3. *The correct answer is C.*
    The Decorator pattern allows for the addition of responsibilities.

4. *The correct answer is C (Chain of Responsibility).*
    You might think this is the Command pattern because of the CommandHandler, but the key to the diagram is the HandleRequest operation in the ConcreteHandler1 and ConcreteHandler2. The Chain of Responsibility allows for the handling of requests by different and unknown classes.

OBJECTIVE: FROM A LIST, SELECT THE BENEFITS OF A DESIGN PATTERN.

5. *The correct answers are A and D.*
    The Façade pattern hides complex subsystems from clients and encourages weak coupling between the client and the subsystem.

6. *The correct answers are B and C.*
    The Singleton pattern controls access to a single instance or a variable number of instances.

OBJECTIVE: IDENTIFY THE DESIGN PATTERN, ASSOCIATED WITH A SPECIFIED J2EE FEATURE.

7. *The correct answer is D.*
    The Home interface of an EJB is a Factory pattern.

5

Security

Security is an important feature of any serious application. This is true regardless of whether the application is connected to the Internet, although the Internet-connected application is probably subject to more undirected and unmotivated attack than a non-Internet connected application. This is because many malicious troublemakers use the Internet to attack systems for no other reason except the desire to prove that they can. However, even though this is the case, a large part of the financial damage associated with computer crime results from attacks specifically against a particular company, web site, or even private individual. Even more damage originates inside the victim organization. Because of the multitude of threats, it is extremely imprudent to contemplate creating any kind of system without deciding how to protect its security.

After completing this chapter, you will be able to meet the following J2EE Architect exam objectives:

- Select, from a list, the security restrictions that Java 2 environments normally impose on applets running in a browser.
- Given an architectural system specification, identify appropriate locations for implementation of specified security features, and select suitable technologies for implementation of those features.

Introduction

The exam has two objectives on the topic of security. These objectives are not designed to make you a security expert, but rather to ensure that you can understand security issues sufficiently to participate in discussions with experts, that you avoid some of the more fundamental mistakes that might result in a particularly insecure application, and that you have a basic understanding of the security controls that the Java programming language imposes on applets running in a browser.

The first objective addresses the constraints applied to applets. This is relevant even if you don't use applets because if you understand what applet security protects you against, and why, then you also have a level of comprehension of some risks that all hosts face. The second objective requires you to have a general familiarity with the technology and terminology of security.

You must recognize that this chapter cannot make you a computer security expert. Rather, you will be exposed to the main ideas, the concepts, and the terminology. If all goes well, you can participate in discussions with security gurus and understand the bulk of what they are saying. As additional reading, the following books and references can add to your ability to make sound decisions, and help you to know when you're in over your head and should call someone expensive to help.

- *Firewalls and Internet Security: Repelling the Wily Hacker.* Cheswick, William R. and Bellovin, Steven M. Addison-Wesley Publishing Co, 1994. ISBN: 0201633574
- *Intranet Security: Stories from the Trenches.* McCarthy, Linda. Prentice Hall. 1997. ISBN: 0138947597
- *Applied Cryptography: Protocols, Algorithms, and Source Code in C.* Schneier, Bruce, 2nd Edition. John Wiley & Sons. 1995. ISBN: 0471117099

- *Practical UNIX and Internet Security.* Garfinkel, Simson, and Spafford, Gene. O'Reilly & Associates. 1996. ISBN: 1565921488
- *Cuckoo's Egg: Tracking a Spy Through the Maze of Computer Espionage.* Stoll, Clifford. Pocket Books. 2000. ISBN: 074311463
- CERT advisories, `http://www.cert.org/contact_cert/certmaillist.html`
- Crypto-gram, the newsletter of Counterpane Internet Security, Inc. `http://www.counterpane.com/crypto-gram.html`

Prerequisite Review

This chapter discusses security issues in terms that require no prior understanding. As such, no specific prerequisites apply, although you should appreciate the fundamental goals of security, which are: protection of data from unauthorized reading or modification, protection of computer resources against unauthorized use, and guaranteeing correctness and availability of resources and data for authorized persons and entities.

5.1 Downloaded Code, Applets, and the Java Security Manager

You probably have heard discussions about what applets can do in a Java-enabled browser. These discussions often gloss over one important point. Java doesn't apply security rules specifically to instances of subclasses of the `java.applet.Applet` class. Rather, it uses a security manager to apply rules to all classes. Different rules are applied to different classes depending on where the particular class was loaded from, and what, if any, signature was associated with it. Generally, the security manager applies restrictions to all classes except those that are loaded from the system's *boot classpath*. The boot classpath is the list of locations from which core classes are loaded. Usually, this is restricted to the jar-files in the directory `jre/lib` under the main Java installation.

This discussion suggests that classes loaded from the local file system using CLASSPATH are still subject to security rules, but you have written programs that open files successfully. You probably know, or can guess, that opening arbitrary files is something that the security manager would normally prohibit. How can your program, which is not loaded from the boot classpath, succeed in opening the file if the security restrictions apply to all nonsystem classes? In a Java application, the security manager is not installed unless you deliberately install it. Installing the security manager can be done in the program [using `System.setSecurityManager(new SecurityManager());`] or from the command line [using `java -Djava.security.manager`]. If code is running in a browser, it is important that the security manager should be installed by default, and that is handled by the browser itself.

What Does the Security Manager Prohibit?

The exam requires you to know the default behavior of the security manager in a browser. This is valuable for two reasons: first, you will know immediately if an applet can perform any particular operation without additional privilege, and second, you gain some understanding of why these operations might be harmful. Don't forget that if an applet cannot perform a given operation by default, then in practice you should probably assume that an applet is not a suitable choice for this functionality because most browser users are unwilling, and possibly unable, to grant additional permissions to an applet.

The security manager works by checking whether a particular permission is granted to the requesting class. A permission is represented by a class describing the general permission. Instances of the permission class describe the permission in more detail by adding a name and an action. The name and action are optional in some permission classes, but when used, they qualify the exact behavior that is to be allowed. For example, the permission class `java.io.FilePermission` can be granted with the name "read" and the action "/tmp/*". This grants permission to read any file in the /tmp directory (but not subdirectories).

The permission mechanism is extensible, so you can add new permissions that control access to devices or behavior you create, and verify whether they have been granted at run time. The exam is not concerned with arbitrary permissions because these are denied to downloaded code by default. Consequently, you need to concern yourself only with the permissions that are part of the core JDK. For the exam, you do not have to learn every permission, with all its variants. Instead, you should consider the categories of permission that are permitted and those that are denied. Also, bear in mind that the permissions change (that is, new ones are added) from time to time with new releases of the JDK.

PERMITTED OPERATIONS

In general, few permissions are granted to untrusted code; typically, only those permissions needed for a program to work, such as the ability to create a thread, the limited ability to manipulate threads in the thread group that the browser created for the applet, the ability to perform essential manipulation of the AWT event queue so that a GUI operates correctly, and the limited ability to read but not modify some system properties. In addition to these permissions, an applet is generally permitted to make network connections to the host from which it was loaded. You might wonder why the applet is prevented from connecting to other hosts. There are two reasons, one more subtle and probably more important than the other. If an applet could make arbitrary connections to any hosts, then applets could be used as the origin for denial of service attacks against other systems. However, the original reason that arbitrary network connections are prohibited is simply that many systems grant privileges to network requests based on the origin IP address of that request. If an applet could connect to arbitrary hosts, it would be possible for it to connect to a server inside your corporate network. If that server grants access to your machine based on IP address, then it will grant access to the applet, because it is sending requests from your machine. The applet could then obtain sensitive information and pass it back to its author, which you do not want to allow.

DENIED OPERATIONS

In general, any operation that might be used to compromise the host is denied. The only exceptions to this are CPU usage, memory usage, and network bandwidth usage. In the security system at the time of writing, there are no checks to determine if an applet is trying to use excessive amounts of CPU time. On most UNIX operating systems, this is not a significant issue, because the amount of CPU available to the browser is restricted by the operating system. On other systems, however, an applet could deliberately create so many threads that the host system, rather than only the browser, becomes crippled.

In a similar way, the use of memory by an applet is not restricted by the security system. The expectation is that the host operating system guards against any single process becoming excessively greedy. Again, it is possible that on some systems this might not be the case.

Finally, use of network bandwidth is not restricted, making it possible for an applet to connect to the host from which it was loaded and start sending network packets as fast as it can. This would degrade the network performance of the host that runs such an applet.

None of these forms of behavior cause permanent damage, rather they are irritating and can generally be stopped by killing the browser that is running the rogue applet. It would be more serious if an applet could access files on the host computer, or execute arbitrary programs, or send network messages to any arbitrarily chosen host. It is these functions that are universally guarded by all versions of all browsers, and have been so since the first time an applet was run.

Because an applet can send information over the network to its originating host, an important goal of the security system is to prevent applets from accessing potentially sensitive information. For example, although an applet can read keystrokes that are sent to it, it should not be able to read keystrokes that are intended for other parts of the browser or other programs running on the host system. Although applets can make normal TCP/IP connections only with the host from which they were loaded, it is possible for them to send data to any cooperating host on the Internet. This can be achieved in a variety of ways, but usually the techniques involve the use of common Internet protocols or services, such as DNS.

Java WebStart is another technology that is available for thin client systems. It becomes part of the core distribution of JDK with the advent of JDK 1.4. Java WebStart provides all the benefits of applets and addresses the problems that make applets less than satisfactory. At the time of writing, there are no objectives that relate specifically to Java WebStart; however, it is a powerful and elegant technology that simplifies corporate system maintenance and thereby enhances security. Any company that uses internal applications is likely to benefit from using Java WebStart. Therefore, it seems reasonable to include a brief outline of this technology, partly because the objectives related to the technology might be added to the exam in the future.

Java WebStart provides a small window that presents icons in a manner similar to a Windows desktop. These icons do not necessarily describe installed applications, but are typically links to code on a Web server somewhere.

When you launch one of the applications shown in the Java WebStart desktop, the classes needed to run that application are downloaded from the Web server. This behavior is similar to that of an applet. However, once downloaded, the classes are stored locally. This allows for a faster startup on subsequent uses of the application. Better yet, each time you try to run that application, the system checks to see if any updates are available on the Web server, and if any updates exist, just the needed changes are downloaded. This ensures that the application is always ready to run, even if your computer is not connected to the network, while also ensuring that the most up-to-date version possible is used. All this occurs with no need for an installation phase.

From the point of view of this chapter, the most significant feature of Java WebStart is that it provides a modified sandbox model. Specifically, the security manager used in Java WebStart does not necessarily reject any request for privileged behavior. Rather, it can be configured easily by either the system administrator or the user to allow such behavior when it is deemed appropriate.

5.2 Foundations of Security

The essential point of security is to protect resources from unauthorized access. This requires two categories of protection: data on the network, and both data and processes on the computer itself.

Protecting an individual computer is usually addressed by the following familiar steps:

1. Determine who wants to do something (for example using a login name)
2. Determine if the person is really who they claim to be (for example using a password)
3. Determine if the person should be doing this (for example using a permission list)

Where the network is concerned, you must address another problem. Requests that are made over the network are usually subjected to a similar type of validation as was just discussed, but in addition, you must assume that messages sent over the wire are visible to people other than just the person making the request. This often requires an additional level of security to disguise these messages so that they are not useful to, and cannot be forged by, snoopers.

Before this discussion proceeds, you must ensure that you are familiar with the terminology that is defined in the following paragraphs.

Consider first the discussion about protecting a computer—the "someone wants to do X, do we let them" discussion. In general, it might not be an individual human to whom a particular privilege is or is not granted. It might be a job function (for example, system administrator or HR director), or it might be another computer or process. In security, the notion of "some identifiable person, function, or thing" to which a privilege might be granted is called a *principal*. Job functions are sometimes called "roles," and many systems, including J2EE application servers, provide a mechanism to list all principals that have a particular role. Most systems have a list of principals. Within the system, each of these principals have some identifying code that is used to indicate for which principal a job is being performed, or to which principal a piece of data belongs. This code, which is often a number, is a method of *identification*.

When a request is made to do a particular job in the name of a given principal, some effort must be made to determine if the requester is in fact that principal. This is known as *authentication* and is often done by using a password. In a login mechanism, a human presents a login name (which is translated internally to an identification code of some sort) as identification, and then presents a password as authentication.

Once an authenticated identification is available, the system must determine if the requesting principal should be permitted to do the work requested. This is called *authorization*.

For the authorization mechanism to have value, there must be a way to enforce the rules that are determined to be appropriate. This requires some form of *access control*, or *resource access control*. To be effective, the resource access control mechanism must be based on features of the host operating system that have been designed for this purpose. The security of the Java virtual machine, for example, would be ineffective in a system running on a host that allows any login from any network address without any form of authentication.

The familiar mechanisms of identification, authentication, and so on, can work adequately, although the system fails quickly in some situations. Imagine that a user has logged in and then leaves the terminal unattended. It is possible for a passer-by to use the terminal and enter commands for which that person is not authorized but the logged-in user is. This problem becomes more serious when a network is involved. Consider the situation in which a message is received on the network; the message requests that a certain file be opened and its contents be sent to the requester. How can the system know if the operation should be performed? How can the data that are sent back be available only to properly authorized recipients. These, and other similar problems, are the purview of cryptography, which is the topic of the next section.

5.3 Cryptography

Cryptography is the name given to techniques that allow information to be modified so that it can pass through public view while enroute to a recipient, but cannot be returned to its original form by the public. There are two distinct forms of cryptography in common use: symmetric and asymmetric, and while there's quite a lot in common between the two forms, they also have significant differences.

In symmetric cryptography, the sender and legitimate receiver of information share the secret of how information sent between them is disguised. On closer consideration, this disguising mechanism typically has two parts: an algorithm that defines what mathematical operations are to be performed to encrypt the data, and also a key. Although you don't typically advertise the algorithm you use, it isn't considered an important part of the security of your system. The key, by contrast, is definitely important. You probably tried this kind of cryptography as a kid in school, for example changing each letter of a message by moving it a certain number of places in the alphabet. In such an example, the algorithm is "substitute the letter in the message with the letter that is <<key>> positions further along the alphabet, starting back at A if you run off the end at Z while counting the positions." Here, the key is the number of positions you move along the alphabet. In all such systems, the uniqueness of the key allows multiple pairs of sender and receiver to use the same algorithm without being able to read messages intended for other recipients. These systems are fairly simple to understand conceptually (although probably not in their mathematics). They are also effective under the appropriate conditions, and are fairly undemanding on the CPU running these systems.

Asymmetric cryptography also involves algorithms and keys. However, in this case, two different, but related keys are used at each end of a communication. One, called a private key, is kept secret, while the other, the public key, is available for anyone to see. There are two important concepts about asymmetric cryptography. First, one key cannot be used to deduce the other. Second, if one key is used to encrypt a message, then the other must be used to decrypt it. This scheme has important consequences. One of which is that if you pass one key out to the world while keeping the other one secret, then anyone can send you a message knowing that you alone can read it. This is because only one key is in the public domain, and that key can't be used to create the other key, nor to decrypt the message that it encrypted.

At first, the notion of encrypting a message but not being able to reverse the process given the encryption key sounds somewhat improbable. It's hard to imagine mathematics that are easy to do one way, but close to impossible to reverse, but that's the way it is. Consider that multiplication is generally easier than division although each is the inverse of the other. Finding the square of a number is significantly easier than finding a square root (assuming you do the operation by hand, rather than with a calculator). There are other operations that are massively harder to reverse than to do initially and these provide the basis for asymmetric cryptography. In reality, there is a relationship between the private key and the public key. After all, the public key is a pair with the private key; in fact the two are usually generated as part of a single process from a single number. The secret to the success of public key cryptography, however, is that it is so very difficult to derive one key from the other. The degree of difficulty is such that it might take a year or two for a cluster of good computers to perform the calculation. This type of operation is referred to as *computationally intractable*. This means that cryptographic systems do not actually prevent unauthorized people reading messages, rather cryptographic systems make it expensive and/or time consuming for them to do so. The idea is to make it so expensive that it ceases to be worthwhile to do so, or so time consuming that the data will have lost its value by the time the bad guys can read it. The quality of cryptography should reflect the value and longevity of the secrets that cryptography is being used to protect.

The public key gives asymmetric cryptography its other, perhaps more common name *public key cryptography*. Public key cryptography is typically many times more demanding than symmetric cryptography on the CPU of the system that performs the encryption. For this reason, you usually try to do bulk communication with symmetric cryptography, and send as little data as possible using asymmetric cryptography.

To recap; public key cryptography is a technique that allows you to publish a public key for the whole world to see. The world can then use this to encrypt a message, but not to decrypt it nor to deduce the private key. Anyone, regardless of whether you've met them, can then send you a message, and you alone can read it This is a useful capability, but you can use these tools to provide even more utility.

5.4 Signatures and Certificates

The public and private keys used in asymmetric cryptography are created as a matched pair. In fact, there is usually nothing mathematical about them that makes one public and the other private. This distinction reflects nothing more than your choice to keep one and give the other away.

Because the two keys are both capable of the same mathematical tricks, it's possible for you to encrypt a message using the key that you kept (the private key). If you do so, then the rest of the world can read the message using the public key that you gave away. How can this be of any value, if the whole world can read it? Well, the point is that if a message decrypts successfully using a given key, then it must have been created using that key's corresponding key. So, if the message decrypts properly with a given public key, it must have been created using the private key that is a pair with the public key that is available to everyone. This suggests that the message originated from the holder of the private key. For practicality's sake you don't encrypt the whole message, but a representative portion of it called a message digest. The idea is pretty much the same, however.

Actually, the reality is not quite as simple as the math. Let's say that Alice receives a message, apparently from Bob. Alice successfully decrypts the message using a given public key. She now knows that the message was encrypted using a key that is a pair with the one she holds. However, that isn't quite the same as saying she knows that Bob wrote the message. Think about the key that she holds. How does she know where it came from? If it was given to her by someone claiming to be a friend of Bob, then she doesn't really know if the supposed friend is playing a trick on her (or Bob) by substituting his own public key and sending a bogus message. On the other hand, if Alice knows that the public key she holds came from Bob (perhaps Bob gave it to her personally) then she knows with the same assurance that Bob wrote the message, right? Well, nearly. What she actually knows now is that the message was encrypted using Bob's key. This might mean that Bob sent the message, or it might mean that Bob let the key slip out of his safekeeping and that someone has a copy of it, or even that there is a trojan-horse program on his computer and that program stole his key and used it without his knowledge. These particular problems can't really be addressed by mathematics, they are is more in the category of social problems.

If you ignore the (actually very real) problem of people not keeping their keys safe, then you're left with the more manageable problem of how to verify that the public key you hold actually belongs to the person to whom you think it belongs.

In the first instance, this problem boils down to a physical issue. If you receive the key by a means that you trust, then you can place an equivalent level of trust in the key. For a single key, this might not be too big of an issue. Alice might take the trouble to visit Bob so they can exchange keys in person, but she's not likely to do this with all the people she wants to communicate with, and the companies she wants to do Internet business with, and so on. However, if she can get one key with sufficient confidence, she can use this situation to allow her to place some trust in other keys.

The idea is: Alice gets one key the hard way. This key is the key of a company that specializes in verifying other people's keys. This company is called a Certificate Authority or CA. The CA makes a promise to Alice (and anyone else who is interested) that they will verify each key that comes to them. Exactly how they do the legwork (asking to see driver's licence, taking DNA samples, whatever) is the subject of a document called the Certification Practice Statement (CPS). When a person (say Bob in this case) has paid the CA, presented his public key, and proven his identity in the way specified by the CPS, then the CA gives Bob a signed message that states "XYZ is the public key of Bob, who lives at ABC." This message is called a *Digital Certificate*, or simply *Certificate*. Now, Bob can send Alice this certificate, and Alice can verify—using the key she picked up personally and at great inconvenience from the CA— that the certificate is genuine. She can then infer that the key listed in the certificate as belonging to Bob is also genuine. Make sense? It's a chain; you have one known good key. That allows you to determine that the other key was seen by the company that owns the known good key. Because you trust that company, you can trust the other key.

Actually, there are still some weaknesses here that you should consider.

First, almost no one gets a key from a CA by anything even remotely resembling a secure path. It is normal to get a Web browser with the keys of popular CAs already installed. This could be a problem if you get your Web browser distribution from a convenient, but untrustworthy, third party. It might contain keys that claim to be from a given CA, but that are actually from someone who wants to trick you. Remember that the whole show depends upon a chain of trust. Weaken any one link in that chain and the whole chain is weakened.

The second problem is with the CPS. Most CAs provide a number of different "strengths" of CPS. To go along with these, they typically hand out certificates of different "strengths." Now, most people don't know that certificates of different grades exist, and even if they do, they often don't know the CPS associated with each grade. Consequently, it is normal to take a certificate at face value, without necessarily knowing if it was issued on the strength of DNA tests, photo ID, or the fact that payment cleared satisfactorily. Recently, one of the major CAs succeeded in issuing a certificate in the name of the Microsoft Corporation to someone who was not representing that company. Obviously, the CPS was not strong enough in that case.

This leads to the third problem. When a certificate is issued, it appears to be genuine until the expiration date on the certificate. Suppose that you paid a great deal, and underwent DNA tests, and you now have the strongest certificate available. Now, someone steals your private key—the one for which your certificate describes the public key. This can happen quite easily, for example, you might keep it on a laptop computer, and have that stolen. You might suffer a virus infection that sends all your files to another host. You might have a backup tape lost or stolen. By whatever means, your private key has been compromised. Now, the thief can send messages signed with that private key, and those messages look to the world as if you sent them. In some countries, that digital signature could even get you a jail sentence, because it's assumed to be valid, and if it has been used on some document that demonstrates involvement in illegal activity, you are responsible for proving that you didn't send the message.

To mitigate this problem, most CAs provide a revocation list (CRL). A CRL enumerates all certificates that have been reported as compromised. An enhancement of this idea is an Online Certificate Status Protocol (OCSP) responder that allows automatic checking of the list. However, this won't help if you don't know about the theft, or if you don't find out about it soon enough, or if the recipient of messages that are supposed to be from you doesn't check the revocation list.

It pays to take care of your keys, and one important approach to this is to avoid allowing your keys to be stored on a computer. A private key must usually be present in the computer while that key is being used for encryption or signature generation, but that time should be kept to a minimum. You can store keys in smart cards, and arrange for those keys to be used *insitu* on the smart card. This approach significantly reduces the chance of keys being compromised.

5.5 Common Tools for Building a Secure Distributed System

Based on the cryptographic ideas just described, you can design solutions for a number of the security issues that surround distributed systems. This section describes those solutions, so you will have a clear idea of the application of, and some of the pitfalls surrounding, such systems.

Secure Sockets Layer (SSL)

Probably the most obvious security problem is that data passed over the Internet is notoriously public. That is, for the most part, you should assume that any data transmitted over the Internet are readily visible to anyone who wants to see them. It is fairly easy technically, although illegal, to get copies of data that are transmitted in this way. The solution to this particular problem is encryption.

As outlined earlier, there are two main categories of encryption that are in common use, symmetric and asymmetric. Symmetric encryption suffers from the need for the sender and receiver to share a secret. This seems like a fairly substantial stumbling block when dealing with someone you do not know, and have never met. However, there are two convenient ways to address this problem. If either party has taken the trouble to obtain a public key certificate, then the other party can use that key to encrypt messages to the first party. These messages can themselves include a new key for either a symmetric or asymmetric encryption algorithm.

Usually asymmetric encryption is used to pass symmetric encryption keys between parties. Once both parties share a symmetric encryption key, they can use that key and an appropriate symmetric encryption system. This is better than continuing with the asymmetric encryption because, for a comparable degree of security, symmetric encryption algorithms are usually mathematically much less demanding, reducing CPU load and speeding up communications.

There are other ways for two parties that have never met to share symmetric encryption keys over an insecure network. The most common of these is called the Diffie-Hellman key exchange. This is an ingenious piece of mathematics that allows two parties to "invent" a key between themselves, by passing a small amount of data from each to the other. However, even if both bits of data that are sent are intercepted, a third party cannot rebuild the key.

With all these ways to exchange keys and encrypt messages, there should be an agreement about how the encryption is performed, what keys are needed, and how those keys are exchanged. It would be even better if that mechanism existed at a library level so that applications could use these facilities without each application having to be programmed individually for this functionality. SSL is a framework that specifies how two hosts connect, pass certificates between one another, negotiate what keys to use, and decide on an encryption mechanism. At this time, SSL is the de-facto standard for all Internet-based secure communications.

The SSL standard, currently Internet Engineering Task Force (IETF) Transport Layer Security 1.0 (TLS 1.0) based on SSLv3, is not a standard for encryption, but is a framework for negotiating a mutually acceptable set of encryption and key exchange protocols. SSL is not the primary source of security in a connection, rather, the connection security is mainly provided by the encryption algorithms and key handling protocols selected by SSL in its negotiations.

There are two primary ways that an SSL connection might be attacked. The connection can be attacked either through attacking the key or the encryption. If the key generation or exchange is flawed, an attacker might be able to gain knowledge about the key. SSL is directly involved in this process, so the design and implementation must be correct if the key exchange is to be secure. The algorithm, by contrast, is not implemented by SSL, but is a separate element of the system. Weaknesses can occur in either the algorithm or the implementation, although more focus is usually placed on attacking an algorithm, because such an attack only requires access to the encrypted messages, not either of the machines.

Some countries deny their citizens the use of encryption, and others prohibit "strong" encryption, preferring to restrict people to using encryption that is fairly easy to break (such as 40 bit DES). If you connect to a computer in such a country, or one that uses weak or nonexistent encryption algorithms for any other reason, you should not be surprised to find that SSL has negotiated a relatively insecure connection. There is little you can do about this situation, but you should weigh the relative importance of getting the information between you and the other party compared with the cost (financial and otherwise) of that information being read or altered by an unauthorized party.

HTTPS

When transferring an HTTP document, it might be necessary for one or both parties involved in the transfer to be identified to the other. Before a customer provides credit card or other sensitive information to a Web page, that customer probably wants to be sure that the information is adequately encrypted when it is transferred over the wire, and the Web server to which the data is sent is the correct server.

What exactly is this second problem? Isn't it obvious that if you are looking at a company's home page, then it really is that company's home page? The URL at the top of the browser is the right URL, doesn't that count for anything? Well actually it doesn't mean as much as you might think. There are two problems, one technical and one human. The technical problem is: Given the nature of the Internet, it is possible for someone to "hijack" a Web address and present seemingly legitimate Web pages, apparently from the right URL, when in fact the pages are coming from a bogus server. In this case, it would be unfortunate to send a credit card number to the source of the Web page. The human problem is much cruder, but it is simpler to implement, and history shows it's almost as effective. An attacker simply registers a domain name that represents a common misspelling of the site they want to hijack. A significant number of potential customers will go to the wrong site, probably without ever realizing it until they call customer service to complain that their card has been debited, but no goods have arrived.

A related problem affects legitimate businesses running a Web server and taking orders through the Web server. Those businesses must ensure that when they receive an order, they can verify the identity of the person placing it. This problem is essentially the same as the customer wanting to be sure the order vendor's site is real, but seen from the other end of the connection.

When HTTP is passed over the SSL infrastructure, HTTP can use all the features of SSL. This combination of HTTP and SSL is commonly used for secure Internet systems and it has acquired a name of its own: HTTPS. You must distinguish HTTPS from the older, less secure, and less popular SHTTP. Generally, SHTTP is inappropriate in modern systems.

HTTPS provides a communications link that is encrypted if the other party is able and willing to do so. Usually a server set up to use HTTPS offers encryption, but remember that it might not use a particularly secure algorithm. In addition to encryption, HTTPS provides you with the opportunity to use certificates to make a positive identification of the other party, and for the other party to have the opportunity to positively identify you if you have a certificate.

So, in principle, HTTPS solves both the main problems of Web commerce: privacy of transactions and proof of identity of the participants. However, in practice, these benefits are not always a reality. Encryption occurs at some level provided both parties can support this, which is usually the case. However, the proof of identity features occur only if the other party has, and uses, a properly originated certificate, current, and signed by a CA. Some, but not many, legitimate e-commerce vendors have these certificates, and not all customers bother to verify these certificates when they're available.

The logical consequence is that you can send carefully encrypted information directly to the wrong person if the other site doesn't give you a certificate that you can adequately verify, or if you fail to verify a certificate you are given.

WEB LOGINS

In the previous section you saw that HTTPS, when used with certificates, allows both a customer and a vendor to be positively identified. However, usually the customer doesn't want to bother with the trouble of obtaining a certificate. Under these conditions, many businesses simply assume that if the credit card is valid, and the delivery address is acceptable to the credit card company, then all must be well. You probably recognize this technique as the one generally used by mail-order houses, whether telephone or traditional-mail based businesses.

Even when no positive identification of a customer takes place, many systems still use the notion of a Web login to allow them to tailor a client's experience. The customer is given a user name and password over the Web, and is generally required to present this information before placing an order. It's important to recognize that this scheme never really gives a positive identification, rather it provides a degree of continuity between one visit and the next—something along the lines of "I still don't positively know your real name, but I remember the nickname you told me and I remember our last meeting." Rather than providing security to the customer, this is more valuable to the vendor. This mechanism can be used to track purchases and other behavior, such as searches, to collect marketing information and to entice a customer into more purchases.

You can use Web logins to provide some degree of positive identification. If the login and password are provided using a mechanism that can verify the identity of that person, then a degree of confidence can be placed in the identity represented by that login/password combination. What kind of mechanism might provide such confidence? Well, that's a gray scale, in much the same way that it is with the distribution of keys, and similar techniques might reasonably be applied. If you meet your customer in person and give him a login name/password pair, you can have a high degree of confidence in who has the pair (or at least, who had them originally). If you use the postal service to deliver a letter carrying the login name/password pair, you can have a fair degree of confidence that a login that results from that login name/password pair is likely to be originated from someone living at the address to which the letter was delivered, even if not from the originally intended recipient. You must evaluate the security of the distribution medium in terms of how it might be intercepted, and how confident you are that the end recipient is the correct one.

Even when a login/password pair has been correctly delivered, the mechanisms by which they are used are subject to potential attack. The server must verify the login/password pair, so this information must be sent over the connection. Now, sending this information unencrypted carries obvious risks, although it's common to do this. Even when the login name and password are encrypted by the client, you usually store them on the server so that the server can validate what it receives. In this case, you must assume that any successful attack on the Web server also compromises all the user names and passwords.

5.6 Protecting Systems

Cryptography provides an important set of capabilities in a distributed computing environment, but although it has a part to play, it does not provide a complete solution to the issues of protecting systems against abuse or attack. In principle, these issues are addressed by the notions of identification, authentication, authorization, and resource control that were discussed earlier. In practice, these issues are more complex than first described. The following sections examine some of the issues that surround protection of a distributed, Internet connected, computing system.

Physical Security and the Insider

Despite the obvious and newsworthy troubles caused by script-kiddies (usually youngsters experimenting with hacking tools they found on the

Internet), international politically-motivated viruses, and deliberate attacks directed against specific businesses, the majority of computer fraud still involves an insider. Disaffected employees or, perhaps more commonly, ex-employees, go into the systems of their company either to do damage or to steal money, intellectual property, or other sensitive information. No amount of technical wizardry can completely address this, it is a personnel and physical security issue. However, when building any system, you should not ignore such issues—always remember that although it carries less glamour and romance, and typically does not involve technical solutions, these issues should be addressed early, often, and continuously. Your role here is largely to ensure that management understands the issues. For more information about this subject, see the examples in the book *Intranet Security: Stories from the Trenches.*

External Threats

Obviously, not every attack is the carefully thought out plan of an insider. External attacks are damaging from a publicity point of view, potentially expensive both in direct losses and in the cost of repairs, and they are also annoying. These attacks can be categorized in two broad groups; those that take place in real time, with someone or some program actively and continuously sending messages across the network to try to control some part of your system, and those in which a program is surreptitiously sent to your system with the intention that it will take some control at a later time. These two vectors involve different operating practices, but might exploit similar weaknesses.

Real-time attacks generally involve sending messages to your system that resemble legitimate service requests, but that, if successful, give the attacker more access than should be allowed. These attacks range from the simple attempt to guess a user name and password pair to more esoteric attempts to break the network software of your systems by exploiting a bug. In every case of this category, if the messages do not reach your systems, then your systems remain reasonably safe.

Delayed time attacks are epitomized by the virus. A program that is designed to copy itself onto other systems somehow finds a way onto one of your systems. It then uses that system to start attacking the other systems it finds around it, propagating in a manner similar to a disease. Some viruses are intended to do damage, often randomly, while others install "back doors"—trojan-horse-like programs that allow more, possibly real time, access later.

In fact, the most common form of "virus" at the present time is really an active e-mail payload, it is a trojan horse not a virus, because it comes disguised as legitimate e-mail and uses the recipient to actively help it get into the target system. Once in the target system, it then exploits poorly designed software to wreak havoc when you try to read it. As with real-time threats, if the attack program never reaches your system, then it is unlikely to do damage.

One type of attack cannot be prevented by refusing to accept hostile messages. Denial of Service attacks (sometimes called DoS, or DDoS, Distributed Denial of Service) work by simply flooding the victim's network connections. In these cases, refusing to accept or acknowledge the inbound messages does not help. The only effective protection is to have the routers in the Internet infrastructure recognize the malicious messages and refuse to forward them. This, unfortunately, is hard to achieve because it requires the cooperation of third parties.

Keeping Attacks at Bay

A number of techniques are in regular use that are intended to prevent attacks from ever reaching sensitive systems. The most fundamental of these is the packet-filtering router. This system provides a single point of connection between a group of sensitive systems (the "intranet") and the outside world (the Internet). The router allows packets into the intranet only if they are destined for specifically listed systems on specific ports. That is, it allows network traffic to communicate only with specific server software. This type of approach can be quite helpful, and is simple to install. It minimizes the number of points in your systems against which malicious behavior can be directed and thereby reduces the amount of work required to check that all vulnerable points are as secure as possible. This approach only directly protects against attacks that seek weaknesses in services you didn't intend to offer; however, by reducing the number of points of potential attack, it allows you to focus on securing the services you do need to provide.

Along with being selective about what systems and ports inbound packets can reach, your systems should allow packets into your network only if there is a reasonable chance that the packet's source address is valid. A packet claiming to be from an address that is inside your network has no business appearing from the outside. Given that privilege is sometimes granted based on the source IP address, this type of "spoof" attack must be prevented at the first available point.

These three filter criteria: destination IP address, destination port, and the source IP address are a bare minimum. You should add additional categories of restriction based on the content of the messages, rather than just the source and destination addresses. A system that performs additional filtering is generally called a firewall. Different firewall products can provide different features, but a typical firewall at least includes packet-based filtering and one or more proxy servers. A proxy server mimics the network protocol of a particular service, but rather than providing the service, it inspects the inbound request for validity. If the message appears to be legitimate, then the proxy server passes on the request. If, however, the message appears to be malformed, or contain other unwelcome characteristics, the message is abandoned.

You might ask what is the value of a proxy server. Well, most software is very complex, and with increasing complexity comes a rapidly increasing risk of bugs that lead to security vulnerabilities. Proxy software should be very simple and therefore relatively unlikely to have bugs. Furthermore, because a proxy does not act upon the content of network messages (other than abandoning or passing them on) it is much less likely that the messages can persuade a proxy to execute any nasty behavior.

The behavior of a typical proxy can be understood by looking at an example. Consider an e-mail proxy. This program probably exists in two parts. The first part is a minimal program that accepts incoming connections, and copies the essential data from a request to a file. This program probably runs as a nonprivileged user in a form of sandbox (for example, chrooted, that is: locked into a subtree of the file system in a UNIX environment), so that its access to system resources is as limited as possible even if it is compromised. A second program runs from time to time, looking for the data files created by the first program. When such a file is found, contents are read and if the messages seem to be valid, they are forwarded to the real mail server on the internal network.

Using this approach, each piece of code is very simple, thereby limiting the chance of security vulnerability. Each program has limited capabilities, so that even if it is compromised, the benefit to an attacker is minimal.

A proxy can also perform content-specific filtering. For example, the e-mail proxy might refuse to forward any part of an e-mail that is not plain text, or it might include a virus scanning capability that would recognize the byte patterns of known viruses and refuse to forward the attachment containing the suspect data. Always remember that each additional complexity increases the chance of a bug, but done carefully, filtering based on contents can be a powerful and effective tool.

In addition to restricting the messages that enter your network, you should minimize the amount of software that is installed on any system that is accessible in any way from the Internet. Even if software is not running, it might be used by an attacker as a stepping stone to a goal.

5.7 Topologies for Securing Networks

The way that a network is laid out can greatly influence the vulnerability of that network. For a firewall to be effective, you must ensure that an attacker cannot simply "walk around" the barrier presented by the firewall. In other words, the firewall must be the only entry point to your network. Many breaches in corporate networks occur because someone connects a laptop that has been infected with a virus while connected to a home Internet connection. Allowing systems on the intranet to make modem connections has similar potential for disaster.

You can employ a number of possible layouts to make a network more secure, or more flexible. However flexibility and security are mutually incompatible, and you must balance these conflicting needs when designing a network.

Simple Firewall Installation

Figure 5–1 illustrates a simple firewall installation.

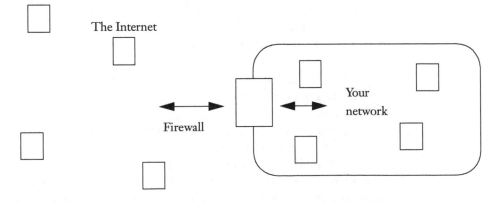

Figure 5–1 *Firewall Installation*

In simple situations, it might be sufficient to build a network that simply uses a single firewall for protection like that shown in the previous figure. In this layout, all messages that pass between any system in the internal network and any system on the rest of the Internet must pass through the firewall. Such a system would be relatively simple to administer, and might provide adequate protection for a network that provides little in the way of services for the outside world. For example, if your network only allows connection from the outside for incoming e-mail.

In the single firewall arrangement, any breach of the firewall's security immediately and completely opens your network to direct attack. This is the main reason that such a simple system is not usually sufficient for a corporate network.

Two Firewalls and a DMZ

Figure 5–2 illustrates two firewalls with a demilitarized zone (DMZ).

Many networks must provide more than one service to the outside, for example, from one or more Web servers. In these situations, where significant parts of your network must be accessible from outside, you probably should use more than one firewall. The layout shown in the previous figure is commonly used to address this situation. It gives a moderately secured area (the DMZ, or "demilitarized zone") that contains externally-accessible services, and a second region that is behind the second firewall. The second firewall is more restrictive and makes the intranet significantly more secure than the single firewall.

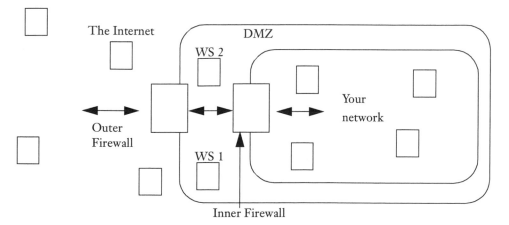

Figure 5–2 *Two Firewalls and a DMZ*

In this approach, the outer firewall allows a significant variety of traffic to and from the services in the DMZ, but little, or typically no traffic is permitted between the inner region and the Internet. In cases where a message must be passed from the inner network to the Internet, it is generally passed through a proxy server that is located in the DMZ. Inbound messages are never sent directly to the inner network but only to a Web server or proxy server in the DMZ. If appropriate, that server might choose to forward the message inside the inner network, or it might format a new request to an inner machine so that it can answer the request that it has just received.

More complex layouts are possible, and in many cases appropriate, but most are some derivative of this form, with layers of protection wrapped around one another. For example, there might well be some systems that should not be accessible to the general user inside the company network. Accounting, payroll, and HR systems usually fall into this category. It's reasonable to create inner protected areas inside the main network for these types of systems. Figure 5–3 illustrates this notion.

This layout begins to address the issues of internal attacks, while also greatly increasing the security of the more sensitive parts of your system.

Each of these configurations shares a number of common themes:

- Firewalls, DMZs, and similar protection mechanisms serve to increase the effort required to break into your central network. This type of layout also serves to slow down an attacker. They should not be considered to be "absolute defense."

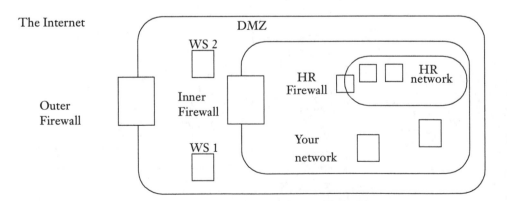

Figure 5–3 *Security-Protected System*

- Nothing should be permitted past any firewall without a carefully thought out decision that the messages are necessary and worth whatever risk they might entail. These decisions should be made by a competent security committee. These decisions should be specific as to which machines might receive or originate which messages.
- Messages should generally not pass directly to any system behind a firewall. Rather, all messages are passed using a proxy. Web servers frequently act as proxies (using servlets and other similar techniques) to application servers and or databases.
- Proxy software should be simple in design and run on a system that has a minimum of services so it offers the fewest possible points of attack. Web servers are considerably more complex than an ideal proxy.

5.8 Monitoring

Many people assume that a firewall is a "fit it and forget it" option; however, this is not the case. You should assume that a firewall-protected network is still vulnerable, although you can reasonably expect that attacking it will take more time.

To further improve the security of a network, you should arrange for continuous monitoring of activity passing through the DMZ. The idea is that if someone tries to break into your network, you have a chance of noticing the attempts before they are successful, and therefore you have an opportunity to protect whatever it is they try to attack. In many cases, that opportunity might be simply to pull the plug on your main Internet connection point for a while.

If you have to look at every packet that passes in or out of your network then you are not going to stand much chance of detecting unusual activity. Therefore, an important key to effective monitoring is to automate the bulk of the work. If the system can notify you when something suspicious occurs, you have a much better chance of monitoring effectively.

There are a number of tools available for monitoring, often built into or supplied alongside firewalls. You should investigate these and compare their capabilities with the types of activities that your network must allow. In addition, you might be able to monitor the behavior of your own applications. A crude but workable example for monitoring UNIX programs would be to run the program under the truss command. You use the truss command to list all kernel calls that a program makes, along with the arguments to the call. If you search that list (using the grep command) for kernel calls that should not be made, then you will spot at least some types of attack.

Perhaps the biggest problem with monitoring is the "false-positive" problem. If a network monitoring system complains that something strange is happening too often, and most of the time it proves to be false, then there is a strong tendency to start to ignore its warnings. This is exactly parallel to the "boy who cried wolf."

5.9   Tunneling

Tunneling is a way of creating a covert channel, that is, a communication path for messages of one type that uses a path actually intended for some other type of message. Tunneling can be used to sneak past firewall restrictions either to get into a network or to get out of a network. Using tunneling to get out of a network might be a reasonable way to behave, but using it to get into a network usually suggests that someone doesn't understand his/her job. The rest of this section discusses these two options to give you an understanding of the benefits and costs of setting up tunneling, and enable you to make a decision about if and when to use it.

Tunneling into a Network

Once a firewall and DMZ has been set up, it becomes harder to add new Internet-accessible services to the internal networks. This, in the first instance is simply because these services are invisible to the Internet as a consequence of the proper operation of the firewall.

To add a new service to your DMZ, access must be granted through the firewall. This might involve opening a new route through the packet-filtering router element of the firewall, and perhaps also adding a new proxy program to the firewall. Unfortunately, there is a tendency for firewall administrators, or the policies created by higher management under which a firewall is operated, to refuse outright any request to open up new access through the firewall system.

When faced with such a situation, there are really only three possible ways to proceed:

1. Decide that the service is not business critical and abandon the project.
2. Persuade the firewall administrators that the service is business critical and convince them that granting access to it is a legitimate business need that they should permit.

3. Use an existing opening in the firewall to create a covert channel to the service that the firewall administrators do not know about.

Option 1 is not likely to be acceptable if your job is to provide the given service. Option 2 might seem impossible from a political perspective. However, as phrased, Option 3 also seems doubtful. You would, in effect, be lying to your own company and deliberately compromising your system's security measures. However, the popular option of "tunneling through port 80" amounts to this behavior.

The primary problem with Option 3 is that security problems do not arise as a result of a particular port being accessible on a particular machine. Rather, the problem arises when a particular service is accessible, and that service has a security vulnerability. By using tunneling, your service is accessible without the permission of the firewall administration. Because of this, the firewall group cannot adequately monitor the traffic, they cannot know if the service needs a patch. In short, the tunnel risks completely bypassing all the benefits of the firewall.

Now, while this is clear in theory, the problem remains that some firewall administrators simply don't understand enough about security to be persuaded by the arguments, and continue to refuse to allow proper access to your service. Indeed some specifically recommend tunneling as the proper way to provide access to your service. If you come across this, which is sadly quite likely, then you probably have to use tunnelling despite the loss of both security and performance that it causes. However, in such situations, you should keep in mind that the firewall administrators don't know about your service, and cannot adequately perform monitoring or regular patching on the service. You should try to ensure that both these functions are performed somehow.

Tunneling out of a Network

Although tunneling is really a solution to a political rather than a technical problem, there are times when the problem is not within your own control. This occurs legitimately when you are writing an applet, or other client, that must run inside someone else's network and needs access to a service that you run inside your own network. Imagine you have created an applet that you want a customer to use to access your services. That customer might be behind a firewall that restricts outgoing messages. You do not have the authority to ask the customer to reconfigure that firewall. In this case, tunneling is a reasonable, if inefficient, option.

Before you set up your applet to perform tunneling, consider whether it might be sufficient simply to run your new service on a particular port, typically port 80. In this situation, you set up your applet and server to operate with their own native messages, but the server listens for connections on a port that is normally used by some other service, such as a Web server. This approach works well if the customer's firewalls only check the destination port number but do not inspect the content of the messages. If, by contrast the customer's system is set up to use a caching/proxy Web server at their firewall, then this approach is unlikely to be of value, because the messages are not in HTTP format, and are dropped.

Essential Points

Downloaded code, such as applets running in a browser, are generally limited by default in the following ways:

- Downloaded classes have no access to the file system. This precludes reading, writing, modifying, or deleting files, reading directory hierarchies, and determining incidental file system information such as the number of files, date and time stamps, file sizes, and file owners.

- Downloaded classes have restricted access to other threads, so the downloaded code cannot block or kill other threads. However, deadlock conditions might still be engineered and, on some host operating systems, threads might make excessive use of the CPU.

- Downloaded classes have restricted access to the I/O system so, for example, they are neither permitted to display a top level window with no warning, nor to grab keyboard or mouse events from other windows.

- Downloaded classes have restricted access to system packages. Classes can be downloaded only into nonprivileged packages and cannot replace or hide any system class.

- Classes live in a partitioned namespace associated with the URL from which a class is loaded, so they can neither interfere with other classes from other locations, nor the system classes.

- Downloaded classes have restricted access to the system properties table, so they cannot determine potentially sensitive information, nor can they modify any such information.

Important security concepts often have key terms or phrases to describe them. These include:

- Principal – A person or entity that is relevant to the security system.
- Identification – Identifies a principal inside the system.
- Authentication – Verifies that a principal is who or what they claim to be.
- Authorization – Determines whether access to a given resource should be permitted to an identified principal.
- Access Control, or Resource Access Control – Enforces the rules specified by the authorization system.
- Private key – A value used in encryption or signing that must be kept secret if the security of the encrypted messages or the validity of the signatures is to be maintained. Private keys are created along with a corresponding public key and are used in those pairs.
- Public key – A value that can be known by anyone. You can use a public key to encrypt messages that are to be sent to the owner of the corresponding private key, or to verify the signature on a message received from the owner of the private key.
- Encryption – The process of producing a modified message from an original message so that the original message can be easily recovered from the modified (or encrypted) message by the intended recipient, but the recovery should be difficult to the point of futility for anyone else.
- Signing – The process of producing a short message (signature) that is impractical to create without knowledge of a particular private key, but that can be identified as correct using only the public key associated with that private key.
- Certificate – A message, signed by one principal (the certificate authority), that identifies the public key of another principal as being valid according to the belief of the certificate authority.
- Certificate Authority – An organization that validates (to some degree) the identity of a person or organization and then issues a certificate carrying the public key provided by that person or organization.
- Certification Practice Statement (CPS) – The statement of the process by which a Certificate Authority decides that a key is actually the property of a person or organization that is asking for a Certificate to be issued.

- Message digest – A short message that can be matched against a particular message, to prove that the digest was created from the message and that neither has been altered since that creation.
- Packet-filtering router – A router that allows packets to pass to only to or from certain ports on certain machines. This arrangement is used as the sole point of access to a protected network from the Internet. A packet-filtering router is a fundamental element of a firewall system.
- Firewall – An extension of the packet-filtering router that provides additional security behavior. Most commonly, a firewall provides proxy services to further control access by the outside world to your services.
- Demilitarized zone (DMZ) – A region between two firewalls so that controlled access from the Internet is permitted by the first firewall only to systems in the DMZ. Access to the systems behind the second firewall is permitted only to the systems in the DMZ not to any systems from the Internet.
- Tunneling – A means of providing a covert channel to a service when firewall administrators will not grant direct access. When used to allow connections out of a network to the Internet, tunneling is a valuable way to circumvent the rules of firewalls that are not in your own control. By contrast, however, using tunneling to get into your own networks should be viewed as breaking your own company's rules, and should be avoided if at all possible.

The following lists corrections to some common misconceptions:
- A signature does not prove that the owner of the corresponding private key read, signed, or approved the document. A signature proves beyond reasonable doubt only that the corresponding private key was used to sign the document. If the owner of the key failed to take adequate care of the key, or the computer in which the key was stored was compromised (such as by an e-mail Trojan horse), then the signature can easily be created without the private key owner's consent or knowledge.
- A message digest does not prove that the message is the original message. All you can know from an unencrypted message digest is that the digest was created from the message it matches. If the message was changed, then the digest must have been regenerated.

- A certificate does not directly verify the identity of the holder of the private key. Rather, the certificate shows that someone who has a copy of what you believe to be the certificate authority's private key believes, or wants you to believe, that the holder of the private key noted on the certificate is who the certificate claims it is. If this sounds like a mouthful, that's because it is. Many things can go wrong here: You might have the wrong public key for the certificate authority, for example if you accepted a copy of it from a malicious third party who substituted a bogus key. The certificate authority might have given you false information, perhaps through malice, or perhaps as a result of having themselves been lied to.

▼ Review Your Progress

This section reviews the objectives described in the chapter and provides review questions to ensure that you understand the important points in the chapter.

OBJECTIVE: SELECT, FROM A LIST, THE SECURITY RESTRICTIONS THAT JAVA 2 ENVIRONMENTS NORMALLY IMPOSE ON APPLETS RUNNING IN A BROWSER

1. *Which would be the most reasonable use for an applet?*
   A. A user interface for an e-commerce system. The front end must perform computation and communicate over the network with the back end web server.
   B. An element of a distributed computation system. Each element must communicate directly with each other element over the network.
   C. A user interface for an e-commerce system that must be able to work in a disconnected mode that allows browsing of a local copy of the vendor's catalog and placing orders for later submission.
   D. An assistive technology system that modifies the behavior of the host user interface by the addition of speech input and output.
   E. A utility that lists all the system properties.

2. *Which ability might be granted to a typical applet?*
   A. Reading a file
   B. Writing a file
   C. Reading a system property
   D. Writing a system property
   E. Setting a thread to maximum priority

OBJECTIVE: GIVEN AN ARCHITECTURAL SYSTEM SPECIFICATION, IDENTIFY APPROPRIATE LOCATIONS FOR IMPLEMENTATION OF SPECIFIED SECURITY FEATURES, AND SELECT SUITABLE TECHNOLOGIES FOR IMPLEMENTATION OF THOSE FEATURES

3. *In a corporate network, there are three divisions, payroll, human resources, and the board, that have special systems. This systems contain privileged data, and this data must be protected against unauthorized access from other parts of the company and from the Internet.*

   As a minimum, what must be provided to address the protections as specified?
   A. A firewall around the three groups as a whole
   B. A firewall around the payroll systems
   C. A firewall around the human resources systems
   D. A firewall around the board systems
   E. A firewall around the whole company intranet

4. *List the issues you would consider if asked to rank the following into order of preference as techniques for obtaining a public key to be used in secure communication with Bob.*
   A. Trent, a friend of Bob, gives you the key.
   B. You find a certificate on an unknown Web site. The certificate signature validates the certificate as issued by a certificate authority using the key installed in the browser you copied from a friend.
   C. You find a certificate on Bob's Web site. The certificate signature is unrecognized.
   D. You receive a certificate from a certificate authority you do not know. You validate the signature on that certificate by phoning the certificate authority to obtain their public key.
   E. Bob gives you both his private and public keys personally over lunch.

▼ Exercise Solutions

The following provides the answers to the exercises.

OBJECTIVE: SELECT, FROM A LIST, THE SECURITY RESTRICTIONS THAT JAVA 2 ENVIRONMENTS NORMALLY IMPOSE ON APPLETS RUNNING IN A BROWSER

1. *The correct answer is A.*

   The applet described in A is a typical front end thin client, for which an applet is a reasonable option. This applet only makes network communication with its own originating host. The applet doesn't need any special access to the local file system, or other privileged resources.

   The applet described in B is described as needing to connect to arbitrary hosts. If the connection could be handled in a hub and spoke manner, using the originating hosts as the hub, then the scheme could be made to work, but as documented, it will fail because of the security manager restrictions.

   The applet described in C would be difficult to arrange because the disconnected mode requires data to be stored on the local system. If the client wants to, then this can be arranged, but it will be prohibited by the default configuration of the security manager.

   The applet described in D would require full access to the window system. The security manager permits only limited access to the window system—specifically to read the events that were directed at windows that are owned by the applet.

   The applet described in E would not be able to list all the values of the properties, because some properties are considered privileged by the security manager. It would also be reasonable to expect any such utility to edit and store these values, both of which would also be prohibited behaviors.

2. *The correct answer is C.*

   Not all properties can be read by untrusted code, but some at least are readable inside the normal sandbox. Modification of properties is never permitted. Normally, no access is granted to any files, for read or write, and thread priorities are limited to reduce the chance of CPU hogging.

OBJECTIVE: GIVEN AN ARCHITECTURAL SYSTEM SPECIFICATION, IDENTIFY APPROPRIATE LOCATIONS FOR IMPLEMENTATION OF SPECIFIED SECURITY FEATURES, AND SELECT SUITABLE TECHNOLOGIES FOR IMPLEMENTATION OF THOSE FEATURES

3. *Correct answers are B, C, and D.*

    As specified, there is no requirement to protect the main network. In fact the only specified requirement is to protect each group from anything not in those groups. That means that the only immediate need is for a firewall around each group.

    In reality, you would not leave the company network unprotected, and there might well be other requirements. However, from the point of view of a precise answer to the question as asked, B, C, and D are the correct and minimal requirements.

4. *In option A, the biggest question is whether you can trust Trent. Even if you know he is Bob's friend, you do not know he is your friend. He might substitute a different key without intending to cheat Bob, but intending to cheat you.*

    In option B, the biggest risk is the use of preinstalled keys in a browser you copied from an insecure source. You do not know if your friend's system might have been subverted with bogus keys for nonexistent certificate authorities. Compounded with the uncertain origin of the key itself, the result is probably a weak form of verification.

    Option C has no mathematical reliability, but depends upon Bob's Web site, and the connection between you and the Web site and whether it was secure at the time you downloaded the certificate. Although the signature on the certificate cannot be verified and it would be hard to recommend this approach, the odds are good that this approach might yield a true key. However, if you intend to use this key for something important you should use a third-party certificate authority to supplement your confidence.

    Option D suffers from the uncertainty about the certificate authority. Phoning them to validate their key, and thereby the certificate, is a reasonably strong approach; however, if you have never heard of the CA, you might just have taken careful steps to prove that the key given to you by organized attackers is genuinely the one created by those organized attackers.

Option E is almost certainly the most sure way to know that you really have Bob's keys. However, if Bob understands the notions of asymmetric cryptography so little that he gives you (even as his trusted friend) his private key, then this suggests that while you have confidence that you have his public key, you cannot have much confidence in the security of his private key. If his private key is indeed compromised, there is really not much that you can assume about any subsequent communications that you might have using the public key he gave you.

6

Internationalization

The World Wide Web (WWW) really does have worldwide reach. Partly as a result of this reach, businesses are less willing to do business solely within their own national boundaries. Therefore, new applications, regardless of whether they are initially designed for Web deployment, must make a deliberate choice regarding internationalization, and the extent to which internationalization might be important to the application both immediately and over the life of the application.

After completing this chapter, you will be able to meet the following J2EE Architect exam objectives:

- State three aspects of any application that might need to be varied or customized in different deployment locales.
- Match the following features of the Java 2 platform with descriptions of their functionality, purpose, or typical uses: `Properties`, `Locale`, `ResourceBundle`, `Unicode`, `java.text` package, `InputStreamReader`, and `OutputStreamWriter`.

127

Introduction

The exam objectives in this chapter are designed to ensure that, as an architect, you are familiar with the capabilities of the Java 2 platform that support internationalized programming. These objectives do not require any significant knowledge of the API from a programming perspective, they only require you to know what aspects of a system might benefit from internationalization, and the broad capabilities of the API. In fact, Java technology provides easy to use and powerful internationalization APIs. As an architect, you should know the capabilities of the API so that you can direct your design team to goals that can be achieved using it. In some situations, if your role as architect extends to that of mentor or team leader for later phases of the same project, a more detailed knowledge of the API might also be valuable. This book, however, does not cover this information.

Prerequisite Review

There are no technical prerequisites to the material in this chapter. You are not expected to be able to program with the APIs that are discussed, but you will need to recognize the purpose and capabilities of those APIs

6.1 System Internationalization

First, consider two pieces of terminology: internationalization and localization. Internationalization refers to creating a program that does not have information hard coded into it that makes it difficult to use in different cultures. Localization, by contrast, describes the process of taking an internationalized program, and configuring it to run in a particular regional or cultural environment.

The primary question that you, the architect must address is always, "what is the cost-benefit analysis?" There is, unavoidably, a cost associated with creating a system that is flexible enough to support multiple languages and cultures. It might be that the customer does not have a clear vision of whether the business intends to pursue foreign markets, or the customer might even believe that the future of the business is entirely local. You should consider the following issue before committing a project to a future that includes a non-internationalized structure: Will the general gain in flexibility be worth the effort, even if the flexibility is not used for internationalization?

Consider this point for a moment. If a program uses the internationalization facilities of Java technology, then it readily supports multiple versions of user interface, multiple functionality sets, and so on. This flexibility can be valuable, even if the output language or target culture never changes. For example, you can use the internationalization capabilities to present totally different user interfaces on the same program. You could use this to allow improvements based on usability studies or to present different versions, with different functionality enabled, to different clients. This is similar to the way the 486SX chip was created by disabling the numeric coprocessor on a 486DX. The technique allows multiple products to be created for a lower total cost, because every product in the line shares the bulk of its code and testing with the rest of the line.

Internationalization requires that a number of issues be addressed in the structure of a program. First, you must identify any aspect of the system that might vary according to the language or region in which the program is being used. Second, you should examine the nature of the potential variations. Finally, you must create a structure that allows the variable parts to be plugged in at run time in such a way that you can add new languages and locales to the finished program without recompiling the whole system. This chapter describes these three issues.

What Aspect of the System Needs Internationalization?

The most obvious aspect of any system that should change when the system is used in other locations is the language. The program might require a change in the text of any messages, labels, and so on. Perhaps less obvious is that program code—algorithms—might need to vary also. For example, different countries have different taxation systems. So, it is important that you recognize that the changes that internationalization might require have a wider scope than simply changing the text of a message.

What Types of System Variations Should Be Supported?

Both code and text will often need to be internationalized. The following is a list of the most common types of changes that you should support.

- Language used for messages
- Parameter substitution order in messages
- Language used for parameters in messages
- Numeric formats
- Date formats
- Dictionary sort order

- Currency symbols and their position
- Tax and other legal rules
- Cultural preferences such as colors and symbols

If the user's language varies, then each message needs to be translated. In addition, changes in language often require changes in word order, and of both numeric and calendar date presentations. Some nations, for example, use a comma to indicate a decimal point, and a period to indicate a thousands separator

Using Java Technology APIs to Create an Internationalized Structure

The type of flexibility required for all the issues discussed, and almost anything else that might be needed, is easily supported using resource bundles, as provided by the class `java.util.ResourceBundle`. A resource bundle is a collection of objects (which can be strings, naturally) that are located using a unique key. For example, you could locate the message indicating a disk failure by searching the resource bundle using the string key "disk-failed." It is important to recognize that the resource bundle can contain any object, including whole user interfaces, and is not limited to textual contents. In fact, the only information items that you cannot place in a resource bundle are primitive types, and even these can be handled using wrapper objects.

A crucial feature of the resource bundle notion is that a bundle to be used is actually selected at run time using a hierarchy searching mechanism based on the locale specified in the environment. For example, if you try to locate a bundle for `TextMessages`, in Quebec, the system will first attempt to load a resource bundle class called `TextMessages_fr_CA`. If this fails, the next attempt will be to load a class called `TextMessages_fr`, and finally, if this too fails, then the system falls back to the default class, which will be called simply `Text-Messages` in this example.

6.2 The APIs

Now that you have considered what might need to be internationalized in a system, you should take a look at the APIs that you can use, and get a feel for what each one does. Although many of the Java 2 platform APIs can provide assistance for an internationalized program, the objectives are quite specific about those that might appear in the exam. For this reason, you consider the following APIs:

`Properties`, `Locale`, `ResourceBundle`, `Unicode`, `java.text` **package**, `InputStreamReader` and `Output-StreamWriter`.

The `Properties` *Class*

The `Properties` class is a simple derivative of the `HashTable` class. It stores objects, indexed for retrieval by a textual key. You can use instances of the `Properties` class for your own purposes in a program, but the Java virtual machine (JVM), at startup, creates and initializes a single instance, known as the system properties. In the system properties you can locate a number of "well-known" values, such as one that indicates the host platform operating system. You can also have additional values set in this table from the command line. For example, if a program is invoked as follows:

`java -Dconfig.option=false MyApplication`

When `MyApplication` starts, it will find the value `Boolean.FALSE` stored alongside the key value `config.option`.

The `Properties` class can also be read directly from a text file, and this makes the properties mechanism especially suitable for local configuration on individual machines.

The `Locale` *Class*

A locale is a representation of a set of cultural and language preferences. It is represented in two, or perhaps three, parts. The first is the language code, and this is considered to be the most significant part. The second part is the country code. The country code adds a "fine tuning" to the localization provided by selection of the correct language. For example, British and American locales both share the language code "en" for English; however, because there are a number of other variations, such as spellings, currency symbol, and the presentation format used for dates, these variations are represented in a suffix to the main language code. The locale name for American is en_US, while the locale name for British is en_GB.

In the Java APIs, `Locale` is a class. Objects of the `Locale` class represent these regional variations, and are used to trigger the most appropriate behavior in a number of other classes. For example, the `Calendar` class uses the instance of Locale that describes the user's preferences to decide what default behavior is required when presenting dates.

The `ResourceBundle` Class

The `ResourceBundle` class is a collection of objects, keyed on a textual (`String`) field. A variety of subclasses of `ResourceBundle` are provided, including one that is easy to set up, but that represents only text in the data part of the lookup table, and one subclass that allows any type of data, but is somewhat more complex to set up. Normally, you would use a `ResourceBundle` class to store all the aspects of a program that might need to vary with locale. Then you would code the program in such a way that it does a lookup, using the key string, to obtain an object that provides the necessary functionality for a given purpose. The significant feature of `ResourceBundle` is that it provides a mechanism to load a particular instance of a `ResourceBundle` subclass (one that you have created for your program) based on a "root" name that you provide combined with the locale in which the program is running. So, for example, if you provide the root name `MyLocalizableElements` and the locale of the host OS is en_GB, the program first tries to load the `ResourceBundle` using a class called `MyLocalizable-Elements_en_GB`. If that fails, then it tries to load `MyLocalizableElements_en`, and finally as the fallback, it attempts to load a class called `MyLocalizableElements`.

The Unicode Text Encoding Standard

The Java platform uses Unicode to represent text. This means that almost any modern language, and a great many ancient ones, can be encoded accurately in a program. Of course, this is not generally enough by itself. The host operating system must be able to display the characters that the program represents. So, for example, if the program refers to a character that represents a Cyrillic character, this displays correctly only if the host OS has been configured with a suitable font. In most cases, however, this means that any Java technology program will correctly read and present the user's native language—presumably the user's computer is set up for the user's language. However, there is the possibility that you could receive a data file from a user in an office that is located in a different country, and while the program might read and interpret it correctly, you might still be unable to view or edit the data. This is not really a problem with the Java technology, or with any particular program. Rather, it is an issue with the host OS configuration.

The `java.text` Package

Different cultures represent information in special ways. Every day information, such as the presentation of dates and the currency symbol, are good examples of these issues. Many of the problems with representing these items have been addressed and have solutions that are built into the classes in the `java.text` package. Specifically, these classes include `MessageFormat` and `NumberFormat`, which provide text layout functionality, and can present many textual items in locally correct form. These items include, but are not limited to, numbers, currency values, and dates.

The classes in the `java.text` package are controlled by an instance of the `Locale` class. Usually, the `java.text` classes will use the default locale object to determine their behavior. However, you can overrule the default locale and instruct the `java.text` classes to use a specific locale if you desire.

The `InputStreamReader` and `OutputStreamWriter` Classes

Although the JVM represents text internally using the 16-bit Unicode, many host operating systems use an 8-bit encoding format that is specific to the user's locale. Clearly, any data entering the JVM, or any data leaving it, must be converted between the 16-bit Unicode and the 8-bit local encoding format. This capability is provided in the `InputStreamReader` and `OutputStreamWriter` classes. As the names suggest, the `InputStreamReader` takes data from an `InputStream` (which is an 8-bit stream) and converts it from a platform-specific format to the Unicode representation. A `Reader` is the Java technology class that represents a 16-bit Unicode input stream.

By contrast, the `OutputStreamWriter` performs the reverse conversion. It takes 16-bit Unicode in through its `Writer` interface and converts it into an `OutputStream` (again an 8-bit data stream) format, using the platform's own local encoding ability.

`InputStreamReader` and `OutputStreamWriter` can make conversions to and from UTF. UTF is a variable length character set that uses 8-bit data (bytes) but might use one, two, or three bytes in total for a single character, depending on the character. UTF actually represents some characters that are not available in Unicode.

Essential Points

The following summarizes the most important points described in this chapter:

- Almost any feature of a program might need to be localized. This is not limited to messages and other UI elements, but often includes algorithms. Common examples of algorithms that need localization are taxation rules, and dictionary sorting orders.

- The `java.util.ResourceBundle` class provides a flexible way of organizing localizable objects in containers. An automatic mechanism is provided that can select the best-match container for a given locale.

- Resource bundles can store objects of any class, including strings, and also including objects that encapsulate behavior.

- The locale used by the resource bundle is typically taken from the environment.

- A `Properties` object allows external configuration information to be read from the command line, or from a configuration file.

- A `Locale` object represents a set of language and cultural preferences.

- A `ResourceBundle` is a collection of objects that can be looked up using a text key. Such objects are typically the locale-sensitive parts of the program, and can represent either pure data or fully fledged objects, with both state and (typically locale specific) behavior.

- The Java virtual machine uses the Unicode character-encoding standard. This allows representation of most natural languages in use today. It is a 16-bit character code.

- The `java.text` package provides a number of classes that support locale-specific manipulation of text, both presentation and input.

- The `InputStreamReader` and `OutputStreamWriter` classes provide conversion of stream data between the host platform's own character-encoding format (usually 8 bit) and the Unicode format used in the JVM.

▼ Review Your Progress

This section reviews the objectives described in the chapter and provides review questions to ensure that you understand the important points in the chapter.

OBJECTIVE: STATE THREE ASPECTS OF ANY APPLICATION THAT MIGHT NEED TO BE VARIED OR CUSTOMIZED IN DIFFERENT DEPLOYMENT LOCALES

1. *Which of the following might need to be internationalized in a program that is intended for international use?*
   A. The user interface
   B. The I/O routines used for reading and writing text files
   C. Binary data I/O routines that write to and read from files
   D. Tax calculation algorithms
   E. The order of presentation of textual lists

2. *Which of the following might need to be internationalized in a program that is intended for international use?*
   A. Encryption algorithms
   B. Icons used for shortcut buttons
   C. Format and contents of temporary files
   D. Presentation of URLs
   E. Presentation of dates

OBJECTIVE: MATCH THE FOLLOWING FEATURES OF THE JAVA 2 PLATFORM WITH DESCRIPTIONS OF THEIR FUNCTIONALITY, PURPOSE OR TYPICAL USES: `properties`, `locale`, `ResourceBundle`, `UNICODE`, `java.text` PACKAGE, `Input-StreamReader`, AND `OutputStreamWriter`

3. *Which of the following provides a mechanism for representing characters from most written languages in current use?*
   A. The `Locale` class
   B. Unicode
   C. The `java.text` package
   D. `InputStreamReader`
   E. The `Properties` class

4. *Which of the following would be most appropriate to indicate how a user wants calendar dates to be presented?*

    A. `Properties`

    B. `Locale`

    C. `java.text` package

    D. `OutputStreamwriter`

▼ Exercise Solutions

The following provides the answers to the exercises.

OBJECTIVE: STATE THREE ASPECTS OF ANY APPLICATION THAT MIGHT NEED TO BE VARIED OR CUSTOMIZED IN DIFFERENT DEPLOYMENT LOCALES

1. *The correct answers are: A, B, D, E.*

A. In this case, it is fairly clear that a user interface will need some degree of internationalization. The messages will probably need to be presented in different languages.

B. I/O routines used for reading and writing text files probably need some degree of localization. Generally, you can do this directly with the `Input-StreamReader` *and* `OutputStreamWriter` *classes, which are already programmed with the details of a large number of 8-bit character set conversions.*

D. Tax calculations is a giveaway. Governments all over the world are notorious for changing their tax rules at regular intervals, and the rules are never the same from one country to the next.

E. The order of presentation of textual lists might seem less obvious, but remember that different countries sometimes have different ideas about dictionary order. In languages that use an unaccented Roman alphabet, the choice is usually consistent. What is less obvious, however, is that this situation is pretty much restricted to those countries that speak English. Almost all other languages have either some additional characters, and or some accent marks. Different countries often have different conventions for the order in which accented and nonaccented characters are placed.

The wrong answer:

C. The only item in this list that is not likely to be subject to internationalization is binary data. In this case, the word binary is the—fairly heavy—hint that the format is predetermined and not subject to the variances of culture or language.

You might think this is an ambiguous question. That's a reasonable interpretation; after all, how can you know for sure what will not need internationalization? The questions in this section, perhaps even more so than in others, are intended to get you thinking. Remember that in the real exam, you will be told how many answers should be selected, so you know exactly how many are right and how many are wrong. All you have to do is prioritize the importance of internationalization to each topic listed and choose the most important "n" where "n" is the number of right answers you have been told to select.

2. *The correct answers are: A, B, and E.*

   A. Encryption algorithms are subject to a number of legal restrictions both in the United States and other parts of the world. For this reason, any program that uses encryption is likely to have to support different algorithms in different countries. Furthermore, it will probably have to support multiple algorithms and perform negotiation to determine which algorithms to use, dependent upon the particular pair of countries that are trying to communicate.

   B. You might be surprised by the suggestion that icons used for shortcuts might need to be varied according to language or culture. However, different cultures interpret the same images differently, and what "obviously" has one meaning in one country might be unrecognizable in another. To add to this, any use of hand gestures, such as pointing or counting, will almost certainly be interpreted as a rude gesture in some country.

   E. Dates are presented in almost every possible permutation in the world as a whole, and many countries even use a completely different calendar. Therefore, any part of a program that presents dates will need internationalization.

   The wrong answers:

   C. Temporary files, such as data files in the last question, are unlikely to require internationalization because they are not used by a human. They store scratch, or working, data and this is generally done in an internal format that is specific to the program.

D. The actual URL, that is, the http://x.y.com/stuff parts as opposed to the pages to which they link, are not generally internationalized because they lose their meaning if changed. Instead, the pages they lead to might be targets for translation, or perhaps different URLs might be provided for different countries so that the user can see the document in their own language

OBJECTIVE: MATCH THE FOLLOWING FEATURES OF THE JAVA 2 PLATFORM WITH DESCRIPTIONS OF THEIR FUNCTIONALITY, PURPOSE OR TYPICAL USES: `properties`, `locale`, `ResourceBundle`, `UNICODE`, `java.text` PACKAGE, `InputStreamReader`, AND `OutputStreamWriter`

3.   *The correct answer is B.*
Unicode is a 16-bit character encoding that provides the characters for most of the modern and ancient languages.

The wrong answers:

A. The `Locale` *class is used as a convenient name for a language and culture, for example en_US specifies the English language, with U.S. preferences for information, such as date and number formatting.*

C. The `java.text` *package provides a number of classes used for formatting messages and parsing input text. These classes actually do the work of formatting numbers and so on. They do this based on a* `Locale` *object.*

D. The `InputStreamReader` *converts from local character encoding into Unicode, but is not itself responsible for representing the characters.*

E. The `Properties` *class is used to store key-value pairs that can specify user or environmental preferences.*

4.   *The correct answer is B.*
The `Local` *class exists to describe a particular set of language and cultural preferences. Because date presentation is a cultural issue, this is almost certainly the appropriate approach.*

The wrong answers:

A. A `Properties` *object is used to store configuration information, and you could use it to store a date preference if you specifically wanted to separate the date presentation format from the other aspects of presentation. However, in most cases, users want dates expressed the way they have been brought up to expect them, and the* `Locale` *object is a better choice.*

C. The `java.text` *package is used to present dates, but it makes decisions about how to perform its presentation based on an object of the* `Locale` *class.*

D. The `OutputStreamWriter` *converts from Unicode into local character encoding. It is not responsible for preparing the characters that it converts, and is not involved in date formatting.*

7

Protocols

7.1 HTTP

7.2 HTTPS

7.3 IIOP

7.4 JRMP

The exam objectives specifically list HTTP, HTTPS, IIOP, and JRMP. These protocols serve two distinct purposes; HTTP and HTTPS are primarily intended as Web page transport, IIOP and JRMP are transports for CORBA and RMI respectively. However, HTTP and HTTPS are sometimes used for other purposes, and IIOP can be used as an alternative transport for RMI. In fact, IIOP is the preferred transport for RMI in an EJB system.

After completing this chapter, you will be able to meet the following J2EE technology architect exam objectives:

- Given a list of some of its features, identify a protocol that is one of the following: HTTP, HTTPS, IIOP, or JRMP.

- Given a scenario description, distinguish appropriate from inappropriate protocols to implement that scenario.

- Select a common firewall feature that might interfere with the normal operation of a given protocol.

Prerequisite Review

This chapter assumes that you are familiar with the purpose and typical uses of HTTP and HTTPS. It also assumes that you understand some aspects of the nature of a firewall, in particular packet-filtering routing and proxy servers. For more information about firewalls, see, Chapter 5, "Security."

You can see that these objectives do not require any significant knowledge of APIs, nor of programming details, rather they focus on the appropriate use of, and issues arising in the use of, these protocols.

7.1 HTTP

HTTP is primarily intended for loading Web pages over the Internet. It provides a number of request formats for the client. The main request formats are called GET, POST, and HEAD. The GET, POST, and HEAD formats are not acronyms, rather they are the actual request strings used by the client.

A GET request is the simplest form of an HTTP request. It carries a single URL into the server and the server should respond with the data for that URL. The URL for a GET request is reflected in the location bar at the top of most browsers. If the request requires any parameters, for example to perform a search, then these parameters are encoded in the URL using a format that avoids the use of spaces or any characters other than seven-bit ASCII. You have probably noticed such encoding, it is often separated from the main body of the URL by a query symbol '?' and the encoding simply uses the hexadecimal code for each special character proceeded by a percent '%' symbol. So, a URL that performs a search for the string "hello there" might look like the following:

```
http://myserver.myco.com/searches text_search?hello%20there
```

This type of request can carry only a modest amount of information into a server request, otherwise the length of the URL becomes excessive. A significant number of attacks against Web servers have exploited buffer overflows resulting from over-long URLs. If you need to pass substantial amounts of data from the client to the server then you should probably use the POST request instead.

As with a GET request, the primary intent of a POST request is to obtain a Web page. However, a POST request differs from a GET request in that it is designed to transfer a significant amount of information from the client to the server when making the request. To accommodate this, a POST request sends the data from the client to the server in multiple lines following the original request, rather than all the data being embedded in the URL.

A HEAD request is used to obtain a limited amount of information about a Web page without loading the page itself. The intention of a HEAD request is to determine if a cached Web page should be refreshed. To do this, the HEAD request returns the date and time associated with the Web page and this can be compared with the date and time associated with the page in the cache.

By default, Web servers, and therefore HTTP requests use port 80. However, the port number mechanism does not influence or control the data that can be passed over the port, so you can use any other port that might suit your needs. For example, you might need to run a Web server on a port other than 80 if you are running a second server on the same machine. Each port can be used by only one process, so the two servers must use different port numbers. Ports with numbers up to 1024 are considered privileged in UNIX systems and cannot be opened by processes unless those processes have root privileges. If you use ports other than 80 for Web servers, the most common choices are 8000, 8080, 8008, and other ports in the range 80xx. Remember though, that these port numbers are not significant to either HTTP, the Web server, nor to the TCP/IP mechanisms.

The port number for any given request is embodied in the URL, and if there is no specific port number in the URL, then port 80 is assumed. Because the majority of URLs loaded by a Web browser are taken directly from a Web page (as a result of the user following a link), using nonstandard port numbers is not usually a problem for the user. However, you should minimize the complexity of any URL that the user might type as a starting point. For this reason, if you can use port 80 for your home page, you probably should do so.

The HTTP protocol is stateless and this sometimes causes difficulty in complex situations. A stateless protocol means that each request/response pair is an isolated, self-contained, unit. Data from an earlier request or response is not available to subsequent responses. This is not an issue when loading simple static Web pages, but is unacceptable in many Web applications. Consider a typical shopping cart application. Some state must be maintained between requests, otherwise it is impossible to associate the contents of one particular shopping cart with any one particular request.

You can add state to a browser connection using one of the following:
- Cookies
- URL rewriting
- HTTPS
- Applets and other clients

Cookies

A cookie is a variable, or name-value pair that is set by the Web server and stored on the browser. The browser can query the value of a given cookie and thereby can associate a new request that a client makes with earlier requests. This allows the server to maintain state across multiple requests. Although a simple and inoffensive mechanism in itself, browsers have suffered from a number of bugs in the implementation of cookies. These bugs have lead to security breaches and as a result some users are not willing to allow their browsers to provide cookie services to servers.

URL Rewriting

URL rewriting is a technique in which the server modifies every link in a given Web page so that the URLs are unique to this particular client. When the browser follows a link in the page, it submits the modified URL and the server can make the logical connection between this new request and the previous one. This technique has a number of weaknesses, but is useful if a client has disabled cookies. One problem is that if a user tries to type in a URL, or keeps a bookmark, then it is unlikely that these URLs will reflect the correct rewriting and jumping to one of them will lose the state. Another problem is that this technique is susceptible to security risks. Arguably, the risks with URL rewriting are greater than those of cookies, because the risks are systemic rather than implementational. Specifically, if a user jumps to a new site, the new site can read the URL of the referring page. Because this URL has been rewritten and includes the state of the connection, it becomes possible for the new server to "break into" the user's connection with the original host.

HTTPS

HTTPS is HTTP using SSL as the transport layer. The SSL connection provides encryption and potentially verifies the parties at each end of the connection, but in the context of this discussion, the SSL connection also provides a maintenance of state between one request and the next.

Using the state in the SSL connection at the application level avoids the security problems associated with cookies or URL rewriting, and enhances security because of the nature of SSL.

Applets and Other Thin Clients

If you can embed an applet into a Web page, then that applet can maintain the necessary state. If appropriate, the applet can open a dedicated connection to the server, using any protocol that suits your needs, and by keeping the connection open, state is inherently maintained. Keeping a connection open has some consequences; each request-response cycle is faster than creating and destroying a separate connection for each cycle; however, maintaining an open connection places some additional resource demands on the server and is unlikely to scale well.

Security in HTTP

From a security point of view, you should be aware of some issues with HTTP. You should consider HTTP requests and responses to be insecure. HTTP sends all messages, both requests and responses, in "clear text," that is, unencrypted. The participants (client and server) are unverified. You might think that failure to verify the server is not a major problem, because the client can see the URL they have loaded, and that URL identifies the server. However, this is not a sound assumption. Because of the nature of the domain name service (DNS), which provides the name/address translation, it is possible to see the correct DNS name in a URL even though you are not connected to the correct server.

Most client firewalls allow outbound connections destined to port 80 on an external server. Other protocols, or perhaps simply other target ports, are often blocked. Most firewalls block connections to unknown ports but firewalls that include proxy servers examine the contents of requests and responses and these firewalls block other services because the messages of different services are not recognized and are dropped.

HTTP is usually able to pass through firewalls so it is a common choice for tunneling. Tunneling is a technique that uses one protocol as the transport for another. So, for example, you can use HTTP as the transport for RMI or CORBA/IIOP messages. A request is encoded inside an HTTP request (usually a POST request) and sent to the tunneling-proxy server, which is a server that mimics a Web server. The tunneling-proxy server takes the request and converts it into the original native request that it issues to the real server. When the native response arrives at the tunneling-proxy server it is then wrapped in an HTTP response that is sent back to the client. The client must create its requests in the HTTP-wrapped format and unwrap the responses it receives. This technique is common, because firewalls are common at the client end and are outside the control of the server administrators, but it is inefficient. You should try to avoid using tunneling; specifically, do not use it in any situation where you are in control of both the client and all firewalls between the clients and the servers.

7.2 HTTPS

HTTPS is not a single protocol, rather it is the combination of HTTP over an SSL transport. Therefore, the properties of both HTTP and SSL are embodied in HTTPS. By including SSL, you gain the following three benefits: encryption, identification of parties, and session state.

SSL provides encryption using any one of a number of protocols. When SSL establishes a connection, it first negotiates which protocol to use. The result should be the strongest encryption algorithm that both ends support. Of course, if one end supports only a weak encryption algorithm, then the resulting connection will be relatively insecure. For systems where the strength of encryption is important, you should validate that the algorithm chosen is acceptable. You can do this either programatically or by asking the user, but consider whether the users will all be capable of making an informed determination.

If a party involved in setting up an SSL connection has a certificate, then SSL can send this to the other party. This allows the other party to validate the identity of the other first party. This validation is not 100 percent certain, although the mathematical process of the validation is close. The weaknesses arise mainly from human issues, such as a malicious third party having copied the private key of the certificate's legitimate owner. Such issues are discussed in Chapter 5, "Security."

SSL connections are stateful, and because of this, HTTPS can support sessions without the security risks of URL rewriting or cookies. However, because HTTPS arises directly from SSL, the connection startup is substantially slower. This is a direct result of the negotiation of protocols and cannot be avoided.

7.3 IIOP

The Internet Inter-ORB Protocol (IIOP), is the protocol used by CORBA systems to call methods and pass the argument and returned data for those methods over the network. CORBA APIs, and with them IIOP, are available for many platforms and programming languages, including the Java programming language. This platform and language independence can be a significant benefit to using IIOP when connecting to legacy systems; however, if you have to install the IIOP support code onto the host of the legacy system, don't overlook the possibility of using RMI directly by installing a JVM on that host and using JNI, after all, the JVM is free and you're probably using it already in other parts of your system.

A substantial body of standard services are defined for CORBA systems, covering a variety of both vertical and horizontal markets. Horizontal services for CORBA include, but are not limited to, naming, security and transaction management. CORBA services are not usually free software though they might be included in a CORBA package. However, if any CORBA services are installed on the local network, the ability to access these might be a significant benefit to using IIOP in your systems.

Java technology systems usually use IIOP in one of two ways, either by using the Java IDL APIs or by running RMI over IIOP. The Java IDL APIs are the most direct way to use CORBA in a Java technology application. Running RMI over IIOP allows most of the coding simplicity of RMI while using IIOP as the underlying transport, and therefore allowing access to any available CORBA services. Running RMI over IIOP also admits the possibility of using both IIOP and JRMP, the native RMI protocols, concurrently on the same network.

Sometimes you might need to run a thin-client program on a system that is not in your own network, for example running an applet on a customer's system. In this situation, it is likely that the alien network has a firewall that does not allow unrestricted outbound traffic. Such a firewall is typically bypassed by tunneling the required messages over another port or protocol that is permitted. Usually, this is port 80 and the protocol is HTTP. IIOP is aware of these issues, and can tunnel through port 80/HTTP.

7.4   JRMP

JRMP is the native transport protocol of RMI. Similar to IIOP, it can invoke methods, and pass arguments, return values, and exceptions over the network. RMI does not typically (at this time) come with a body of services, though there is a naming service included with it. The most significant difference from IIOP however, is that JRMP does not restrict argument and return types to data values, JRMP handles objects. Objects have state and behavior, which means that JRMP provides a mechanism to transfer the class file of an object into the recipient of an argument or returned value (or an exception for that matter). This copying of class file is done on an as-needed basis to avoid wasting bandwidth. Before you can copy classes, you must complete additional administrative setup. Because these setup tasks are sometimes not done, or done incorrectly, you sometimes find RMI/JRMP systems that exhibit the more limited behavior of CORBA, that is, that do not move objects over the network, but only move state. This is not always a problem, provided the system is designed that way, indeed, it can result in slightly higher performance and slightly lower network bandwidth usage.

Because JRMP is the native protocol for RMI and does not have to support a myriad of different host data formats and byte ordering, there is less overhead in setting up the argument and return values for a call over JRMP than with language neutral systems, such as IIOP. Used correctly, this can result in higher performance.

JRMP does not include encryption or identification of parties by default. However, it is easy to set JRMP to use SSL as a transport. This is achieved by using "socket factories." Further information on the mechanics of this is in the API documentation. Additionally, Java Authentication and Authorization Service (JAAS) is a framework for distributed authentication and authorization, and adds a great deal of valuable security functionality to a system.

It is common to think of JRMP as restricted to use with Java technology. This isn't accurate. In the same way that installation of additional code (the CORBA system) on, for example, a C++ system allows that system to communicate using IIOP, installation of additional code (a JVM) allows that same C++ system to communicate using JRMP. Therefore, the appropriate use of JNI allows JRMP to provide its functionality in a language-neutral way. JNI is bidirectional, it allows the invocation of a Java technology system from outside as well as allowing the Java technology system to invoke the legacy system.

If you try to run an applet on a customer's system, and that applet attempts to use JRMP to communicate with one of your systems, then you will quickly run into the problem of firewalls that restrict outbound traffic. The standard solution to this is tunneling using HTTP on port 80, and this is supported by JRMP.

Essential Points

The following summarizes the most important points described in this chapter.

- HTTP can run on any port as needed, although port 80 is the default.
- HTTP GET requests carry a limited amount of data from client to server, POST requests can carry unlimited amounts.
- HTTP is a stateless protocol. State can be added by using cookies, URL rewriting, or using SSL as a transport (which produces HTTPS).
- HTTP on port 80 is usually allowed out of firewalls, so HTTP is a common choice for tunnelling.
- HTTPS is HTTP over SSL
- SSL gives encryption, validation of parties, and an identifiable session for maintaining state.
- Encryption and validation in SSL depend on configuration and capabilities of both ends, and might be negotiated to nothing.
- SSL, and therefore HTTPS, has a significant startup overhead.
- IIOP is the method-invocation protocol for CORBA.
- IIOP moves state for arguments and return values of method calls.
- CORBA defines a variety of standard services that, if installed, will be available to IIOP.
- CORBA services include security, transactions, and naming.
- CORBA, and therefore, IIOP, is available for a variety of languages and platforms.
- IIOP is supported by Java IDL and RMI/IIOP.
- IIOP supports tunneling over HTTP/port 80.
- JRMP is the method-invocation protocol for RMI.

- JRMP moves state and behavior (whole objects) for arguments, return values, and exceptions in method calls.
- JRMP is a native Java technology protocol, so it has less overhead than protocols that have to perform format conversion.
- JRMP can use SSL and JAAS for security.
- JRMP connects to other languages via JNI.
- JRMP supports tunneling over HTTP/port 80.

▼ Review Your Progress

This section reviews the objectives described in the chapter and provides review questions to ensure that you understand the important points in the chapter.

OBJECTIVE: GIVEN A LIST OF SOME OF ITS FEATURES, IDENTIFY A PROTOCOL THAT IS ONE OF THE FOLLOWING: HTTP, HTTPS, IIOP, OR JRMP

1. *Which protocol exhibits all of the following properties?*
   - A method-invocation protocol
   - Can connect to many languages on many platforms
   - Moves objects (state and behavior) as arguments
   A. HTTP
   B. HTTPS
   C. JRMP
   D. IIOP

2. *Which protocol provides for encryption and identification of participants?*
   A. HTTP
   B. HTTPS
   C. JRMP
   D. IIOP

3. *Which protocol normally has a transaction service associated with it?*
   A. HTTP
   B. HTTPS
   C. JRMP
   D. IIOP

OBJECTIVE: GIVEN A SCENARIO DESCRIPTION, DISTINGUISH APPROPRIATE FROM INAPPROPRIATE PROTOCOLS TO IMPLEMENT THAT SCENARIO

4. *Which protocol would be most suitable in this situation:*
   A client will make a request, including a small amount of data. The response takes the form of a large amount of unstructured data. The request is not part of a transaction, nor does this request require any association with previous or subsequent requests. Security is not considered an issue, but response time should be reasonable.

   A. HTTP

   B. HTTPS

   C. JRMP

   D. IIOP

5. *Consider this extract from a requirements specification:*
   The systems at the remote sites obtain pricing and availability information from our central server. In addition, the server provides discount calculation, sale reporting, and similar functions. All systems and all networks at all sites are under the company's control, and this is expected to continue to be the case. The connections between systems are made over the public Internet, but it is important that the network traffic be secure. The remote systems are mostly Microsoft Windows, but a few are Apple Macintosh, the Solaris Operating Environment, or Linux. In the future, the company intends to standardize on Linux or the Solaris Operating Environment, but this transition will take a long time, and will probably not be 100 percent complete for many years. However, as part of this drive, no other types of system will be installed. At the present time no software has been developed for the systems at remote sites. The cost of software, both purchased and development cost, should be kept to a minimum.

   Which protocol would best support these requirements?

   A. HTTP

   B. HTTPS

   C. JRMP

   D. IIOP

OBJECTIVE: SELECT A COMMON FIREWALL FEATURE THAT MIGHT INTERFERE WITH THE NORMAL OPERATION OF A GIVEN PROTOCOL

6. *Rank the protocols in order of likelihood that the protocol will pass out of a customer's firewall, and state your reasons for your choice.*

   A. HTTP

   B. HTTPS

   C. JRMP

   D. IIOP

7. *Your client-side system uses HTTP tunneling to allow it to send messages out of customer's networks. One particular customer, finds that the system does not work for him when using his laptop in his office, although the same laptop works properly when connected at his home. What firewall behavior might cause this effect?*

▼ Exercise Solutions

The following provides the answers to the exercises.

OBJECTIVE: GIVEN A LIST OF SOME OF ITS FEATURES, IDENTIFY A PROTOCOL THAT IS ONE OF THE FOLLOWING: HTTP, HTTPS, IIOP, OR JRMP.

1. *The correct answer is C.*
   Neither HTTP nor HTTPS are method-invocation protocols so A and B must be wrong. Both JRMP and IIOP can connect to legacy code created in a variety of languages, JRMP does so using JNI. However, IIOP moves state, but not behavior in method calls. JRMP can move whole objects including their behavior part. Therefore, C is the correct answer.

2. *The correct answer is B.*
   HTTPS, that is the combination of HTTP and SSL, provides for these features directly by virtue of the capabilities of SSL. It is true that by using SSL as the transport layer for any of the others, or by using security services of CORBA, these features can be added.

3. *The correct answer is D.*
   IIOP is the transport protocol for CORBA. CORBA systems are commonly supplied with a number of standard services, including naming, security, and transactions.

Objective: Given a scenario description, distinguish appropriate from inappropriate protocols to implement that scenario.

4. The correct answer is A.

The observations about the unstructured nature of the data are hints that JRMP and IIOP are not the intended protocols here. They can be used to transfer unstructured data (as a large string, for example), but that is not really their purpose. By contrast, HTTP and therefore HTTPS, specialize in unstructured data, returning anything that is convenient at the time, such as a Web page, or perhaps some MIME extension type, such as an image or audio file.

The information that each request is not part of a transaction is not of great importance, although, if the situation indicated that a transaction support requirement, this would be significant. The comment "does not require any association with previous or subsequent requests" implies that no session state is needed. This, combined with not needing security, means that HTTPS would involve an unwarranted overhead, leading to the conclusion that HTTP, option A is the correct choice.

5. The correct answer is C.

The description mentions a number of functions that must be provided over the wire. Although you can achieve these behaviors over HTTP or HTTPS, distributed computing type functionality is better supported by JRMP or IIOP, which were designed for this type of behavior. Because all the networks are under the company's direct control, there should be no requirement for tunnelling. The need for security can be met by either JRMP using SSL as a transport, or by IIOP using the CORBA security service. The listed systems all support Java technology, and CORBA systems are also available for the platforms. The exclusion of other platforms has no particular significance, but means that you do not need to consider the possibility of a system being added that is hard to support with your choice of transport (not likely given the pro-tocols in question). Because no software has been developed yet, there is no need to interface with legacy code, although both IIOP and JRMP can do this if necessary. Finally, the minimum cost requirement suggests that JRMP would be a good choice, because RMI, and therefore, JRMP, is an integral part of the free JDK distribution. IIOP is supported by Java technology, but it is less likely that you would find a free security service to support it.

OBJECTIVE: SELECT A COMMON FIREWALL FEATURE THAT MIGHT INTERFERE WITH THE NORMAL OPERATION OF A GIVEN PROTOCOL.

6.   *The correct answers are A, B, D, and C.*

Don't panic, you will not get a question like this on the exam. You're right, this is not something for which an absolutely right answer is possible. However, this question is here to make you think, and what matters is that you understand the following discussion.

Many firewall administrators restrict outgoing connections. The usual argument for this is to limit the opportunity for company data to be sent out, either by malicious attackers who have broken in, or by disaffected employees. There are two ways a firewall normally limits such traffic. These are port restrictions and service proxies.

When setting up restrictions, most administrators use the rule "that which is not explicitly permitted is denied." This is a sound and long standing security mantra that means, more or less, turn all traffic off, then turn back on only those elements that you a) think are safe, and b) have determined are required. Unfortunately, tunneling makes the whole notion rather pointless, because any data can be sent out over port 80 in the form of an HTTP request. Nevertheless, this is the approach usually taken, and it is perhaps better than nothing.

The upshot is that many firewalls restrict outgoing connections to a few well known services. HTTP is usually one of them, making A the first correct choice. HTTPS is usually thought of as being used by legitimate e-business, and is quite often allowed. Of course, if you are tunnelling for the deliberate purpose of stealing company data, then HTTPS is a better choice than HTTP, because you can encrypt the content of the messages, and thereby ensure that no one can see that the message contains confidential company documents. In practice, however, HTTPS is the next most likely protocol to be allowed out. Choosing between JRMP and IIOP for the third and fourth options is harder. A firewall administrator is unlikely to allow connections to the ports of either protocol if the firewall is restricting outgoing connections at all, but since IIOP has been around longer, and is therefore slightly better known, it is the third choice. If you chose JRMP third, or perhaps scored a draw between IIOP and JRMP, that's fine too.

7.   *Correct answer: There are all kinds of reasons this might happen; however, the question restricts you to considering firewall behavior.*

Many firewalls provide proxy servers for Web access and HTTP connections. Such a proxy might refuse to connect to certain external hosts, although this is not a strong candidate in this case. Web proxy servers sometimes inspect the contents of the requests and responses that pass through them. In this case, it is possible that your tunneled packets are being rejected. Perhaps the proxy has been configured to reject encrypted data (because it cannot be inspected to see if it contains proprietary information).

Another possibility is that the firewall only allows connections outbound from desktop systems that have permanently assigned IP addresses. Since the laptop runs at home and at work, it probably uses a DHCP allocated address, and that address might be on a list that the firewall uses to reject outgoing connections, or that the firewall uses to perform more detailed scrutiny, such as rejecting encrypted packet contents.

Case Study

Part two of SCEA is an assignment that you complete on your own time. This chapter presents a case study that is similar to the exam assignment. To complete the assignment, you must complete class diagram(s), component diagram(s), and sequence or collaboration diagrams.

8.1 Case Study

Golf Equipment Store (GES) is a golf equipment mail-order company. GES carries the largest selection of golf equipment from every manufacturer.

Within the last year, GES has seen an increase in competition and GES expects that increase to continue. Most of the competition comes from the low-cost retail stores that provide additional services and products. However, GES has a loyal customer base. At this time, they are expanding from a strictly mail-order-based company to one with an electronic business (e-business) presence. GES is trying to transition most of their business to a Web commerce site.

GES has back-office systems in place to support the current operating environment that supports its Web commerce site. The back-office systems are: Accounting, Content Management, Inventory, Payment Server, and Shipping. The Accounting system from Big O Corporation is written in the Java programming language. The Content Management system from Vine Corporation provides C++ and Java technology interfaces. The Inventory system from FIFO Corporation is written in C++ with a CORBA backbone. Payment Server is provided by ePay, which has both Java technology and C++ interfaces. The Shipping system is a home-grown system that is written in the Java programming language.

The current business process is for customers to place their orders by mail, fax, or phone using a catalog that was previously mailed to them. When the order is received at GES, it is entered into the Order Entry system, which deducts the items from inventory, authorizes credit cards, and notifies the warehouse to ship the items.

GES would like to create an online store to allow customers to enter their own order. In addition, they would like to start developing relationships with their manufacturers to conduct business online. To do this, GES needs a system that can meet the following the goals:

1. Maintain current staffing levels of customer service representatives while growing the business revenue by 35 percent each year.
2. Reduce the maintenance costs associated with desktop systems.
3. Provide an electronic-commerce (e-commerce) site for customers.

The business analyst created the following use-case diagram, use-case descriptions, and business domain object model. This is an accurate representation of the system and you cannot modify or change it in any way. You might not agree with the analyst, but you must use this representation of the system.

Use-Case Diagram

Figure 8–1 illustrates the use-case diagram for the GES system.

Figure 8–1 *GES Use-Case Diagram*

Business Domain Model

The following illustrates the business domain object model.

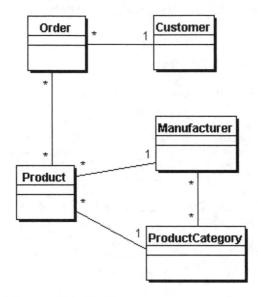

Figure 8–2 *Domain Object Model*

Use Case – Browse Catalog

The Browse Catalog use case allows the customer to browse all the products by category or manufacturer without being logged in. The product and manufacturer information including any images is retrieved from the Content Management subsystem.

BASIC FLOW

The following steps outline the basic flow of the Browse Catalog use case:

1. Customer selects browse catalog.
2. System presents the main page of the catalog that has a list of categories and a list of manufacturers.
3. Customer selects a category (bags, shoes, clubs, balls, misc.).
4. System responds with the top ten items sold in this category and a list of manufacturers that have products in this category.
5. Customer selects a manufacturer from the list.
6. System responds with a page showing images of the different products carried by the manufacturer.

7. Customer selects a product to add to the shopping cart.
8. System responds with a list of selectable attributes on the product. For example, size or color.
9. Customer selects attributes for the product.
10. System responds by placing the item in the shopping cart.
11. Customer selects a quantity for the product.

Use Case – Search for Product

The Search for Product use case allows the customer to enter a product name or manufacturer and see a list of results that meet the search criteria. The product and manufacturer information including images is retrieved from the Content Management subsystem.

BASIC FLOW

The following steps outline the basic flow of the Search for Product use case:

1. Customer enters search criteria, which could be a product name, manufacturer, product category or any combination of this information.
2. System responds with a list of products.
3. Customer selects the product to add to the shopping cart.
4. System responds with a list of selectable attributes on the product.
5. Customer selects attributes for the product.
6. System responds by placing the item in the shopping cart.
7. Customer selects a quantity for the product.

Use Case – Maintain Shopping Cart

The Maintain Shopping Cart use case allows the customer to see what is in the shopping cart and modify the contents.

BASIC FLOW

The following steps outline the basic flow of the Maintain Shopping Cart use case:

1. Customer selects view shopping cart.
2. System responds with the current products that are in the shopping cart.

3. Customer modifies items in the cart by selecting to delete an item or change a quantity, then submits changes.

4. System uses the Inventory subsystem to verify the availability of the product and responds by updating the shopping cart with the requested changes.

Use Case – Create Account

When the customer decides to check out after shopping, the customer must sign-on. If the customer does not have an account, then the customer must create an account. You can also access this use case by clicking the Create Account button.

BASIC FLOW

The following steps outline the basic flow of the Create Account use case:

1. System presents the Customer Account form when the user does not have an account set up.

2. Customer enters name, home address, shipping address, multiple phone numbers, multiple credit cards and requested user ID and password.

3. System validates the user ID and password and creates the customer account.

Use Case – Check Out

The Check Out use case allows the customer to purchase the products in the shopping cart.

BASIC FLOW

The following steps outline the basic flow of the Check Out use case:

1. Customer presses the checkout button/link on any screen.
2. System responds with the Account Sign-on form.
3. Customer enters the user ID and password for the account.
4. System authenticates the user and displays the shopping cart and list of shipping options from the shipping subsystem.
5. Customer selects the shipping option and presses recalculate.
6. System responds with a total amount due and payment methods.
7. Customer selects payment by credit card.

8. System gets credit card approval from payment server, assigns an order number and sends the order to the inventory system.

ALTERNATIVE FLOW

The following describes an alternative flow for the Check Out use case:

- No customer account (Step 3 in the Basic Flow):
  3a. User does not have an account so the user selects Create Customer Account, which calls the Create Account use case and returns to Step 5 in the Basic Flow.
- User already signed in (Step 2 in the Basic Flow):
  2b. User already signed in. In this case the user would go to Step 5.
- Payment by ACH (auto withdraw), (Step 7 in the Basic Flow):
  7a. Checker selects payment by ACH, which changes Step 8 in the Basic Flow:
  8. System sends the ACH request to the payment server, assigns an order number and sends the order to the inventory system.

Use Case – Maintain Account

The Maintain Account use case allows the customer to update account information.

BASIC FLOW

The following steps outline the basic flow of the Maintain Account use case:

1. Customer selects maintain account.
2. System displays the account form load with the Account Maintainer's data.
3. Customer updates appropriate data and submits the information to the system.
4. System updates account information.

ALTERNATIVE FLOW

The following describes an alternative flow for the Check Out use case. In the alternative flow, you delete the account rather than maintain the account:

- Step 3 changes to:
  3a. Customer presses delete account.

- Step 4 changes to:
  4a. System responds with a confirmation.
- There is a Step 5:
  5. Customer confirms the deletion.
- There is a Step 6:
  6. System marks account as deleted.

Use Case – Review Order

The Review Order use case allows the customer to check the status of an order.

BASIC FLOW

The following steps outline the basic flow of the Review Order use case:

1. Customer selects a review order.
2. System responds with a list of orders.
3. Customer selects an order to view.
4. System responds with details about the order.

Use Case – Request Item Return

The Request Item Return use case allows the customer to request that an item be returned.

BASIC FLOW

The following steps outline the basic flow of the Request Item Return use case:

1. Customer selects the return item option.
2. System responds with the return item form.
3. Customer enters item information and presses submit.
4. System writes return item request to storage.

Use Case – Return Item

The Return Item use case returns an item that has been requested to be returned.

BASIC FLOW

The following steps outline the basic flow of the Return Item use case:

1. Customer Service Representation (CSR) reviews return request and approves return.
2. System sends notification to customer and sends a refund request to accounting.

ALTERNATIVE FLOW

The following describes an alternative flow for the Return Item use case:

- If the CSR does not approve the return (Step 1):
  1a. CSR does not approve the return.

- Step 1 continues with:
  1b. The CSR selects the reason for the denied return and clicks Submit.

- Step 2 changes to:
  2a. System sends notification to customer requesting more information.

8.2 Solution

The deliverables for the assignment are class diagram(s), component diagram(s) and sequence diagrams. As long as you supply the required diagrams any other diagrams may be provided without impacting your score. Any clarity you may provide with descriptions and additional diagrams does not add points, but will help the assessor to evaluate your assignment.

Layer Map

The layer map shows the layers of the system. The application layer is where the application code resides with the exception of the common services code. The common services code is code that is shared across many systems in the organization. The upper layer consists of the Web server, application server, and any other infrastructure type software necessary to support the application and common services. The lower layer is the hardware and operating system. Figure 8–3 illustrates the layers of the system.

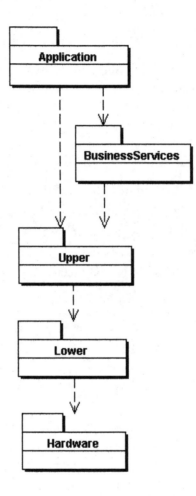

Figure 8–3 *System Layers*

The Application layer breaks down into the following packages: Customer, Order, and Catalog. The Customer package contains the components to create and maintain the customer account. The Order package contains the components to process orders and return items. The Catalog package contains the components to search and browse the catalog. Figure 8–4 shows the packages and their dependencies to the subsystems.

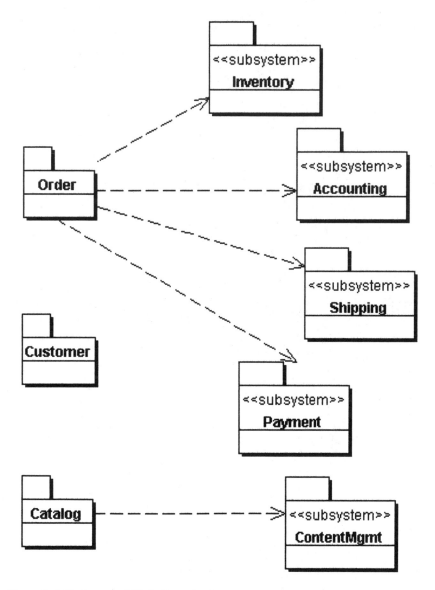

Figure 8–4 *Packages and Their Dependencies*

Tier Map

The Application layer tiers are logical not physical. The logical separation of the application into these different tiers allows a system to be flexible and easily maintained. The Client tier is the point at which the data model is consumed. This tier could be a PC browser, WAP browser, or any other device capable of browsing. The Presentation tier is used to maintain session management and deal with the diverse clients that can connect to the system. The BusinessLogic tier is where the business application processing takes place. Because the system will interface with diverse resources on the backend, the Integration tier handles the creation of the data model from the diverse resources. The Resource tier is where the application data is persisted in relational databases or legacy systems. Figure 8–5 illustrates how the tiers are mapped.

Figure 8–5 *Tier Map*

Class Diagram

The class diagram is a little different from the Business Domain Object Model (BDOM) provided by the business analyst, but it provides additional details and still meets the requirements of the BDOM. The Address, CreditCard, and ShoppingCart have all been added with relationships to Customer. Payment and LineItem have been added to expand the Order. Manufacturer is no longer an object, it is now an attribute of Product. In addition, an Order no longer has a direct relationship to Product, it must use LineItem to form the relationship. Stateless session beans have been added to show the classes that will handle the workflow and business logic rules.

The home and remote interfaces for the EJBs have not been added, because those interfaces have a tendency to clutter the diagram and the developers already know how that an EJB needs a home and remote interface. At this point, attributes and operations have not been added to the classes because that information will be done during the detailed design. This diagram just shows the basic classes that will be used in the system to provide some structure and business rules. A detailed class diagram will be created by the developers during the design of the system. Figure 8–6 illustrates a class diagram.

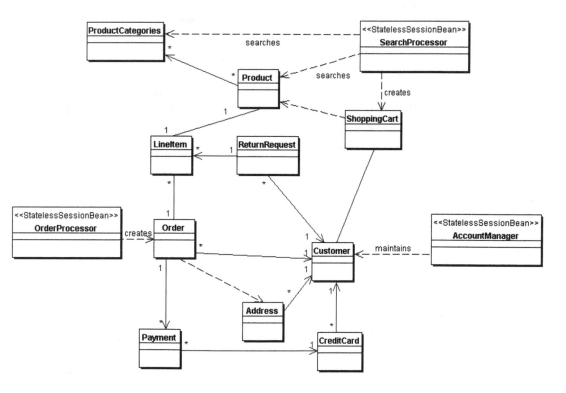

Figure 8–6 *Class Diagram*

Component Diagrams

The component diagrams for this system have been broken down into three separate diagrams. There is one diagram for each package structure within the system. These diagrams provide additional information about the basic structure of the system and how it will function.

The Catalog Component Diagram (Figure 8–7) shows the flow of events that take place between the components to handle the action of browsing the catalog and searching the catalog. The CatalogController serves as the controller for all user interface requests. The ServiceLocator is a class that is used by the CatalogController to find and load the SearchProcessor. This ServiceLocator is contained in the CommonServices package and is used in all the component diagrams.

The Order Component Diagram (Figure 8–8) shows the component flow that should be followed when doing the detail design on the following use cases: Review Order, Checkout, Return Item and Request Item Returnees OrderController serves as the control mechanism for the user interface. The ServiceLocator locates the OrderProcessor, which is the business logic and workflow. The OrderDAO is used to retrieve the order data used in the processing of orders. Because the Shipping, Payment, and Accounting systems have Java technology APIs and the data is not persisted, you have direct access from the OrderProcessor as opposed to encapsulating the requests in a DAO.

The Customer Component Diagram (Figure 8–9) shows the component interaction that should be followed when doing the detail design on the following use cases: Create Account and Maintain Account.

Sequence Diagrams

Sequence diagrams (Figures 8–10 through 8–13) at the architectural level structure the components and dictate a flow of events through the components. These diagrams are not using classes or objects, but components to provide the developer with some guidelines for developing a detailed design of the system. For simplicity, there are two sequence diagrams with a corresponding collaboration diagram. The assignment asks for one or the other, you do not have to provide both.

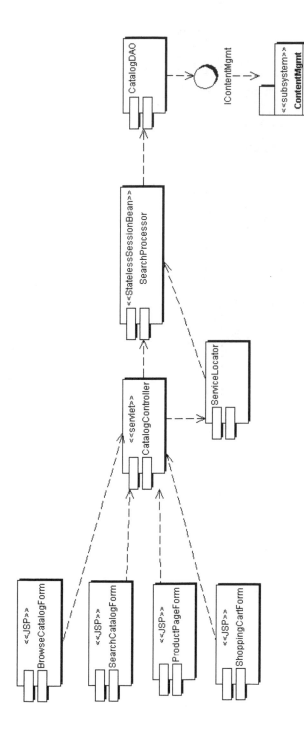

Figure 8–7 *Catalog Component Diagram*

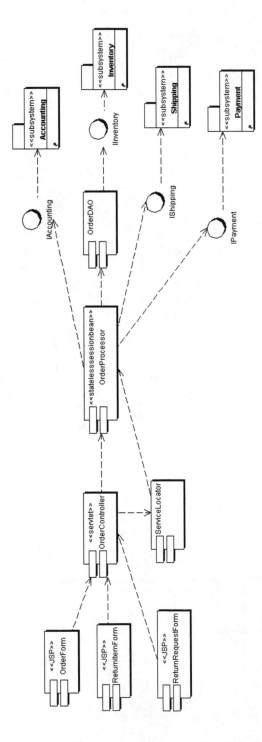

Figure 8–8 *Order Component Diagram*

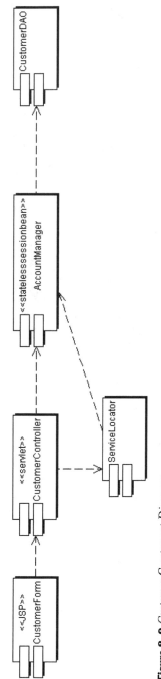

Figure 8–9 *Customer Component Diagram*

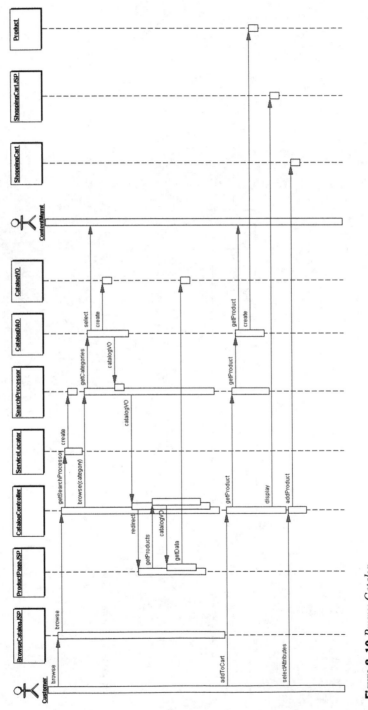

Figure 8-10 *Browse Catalog*

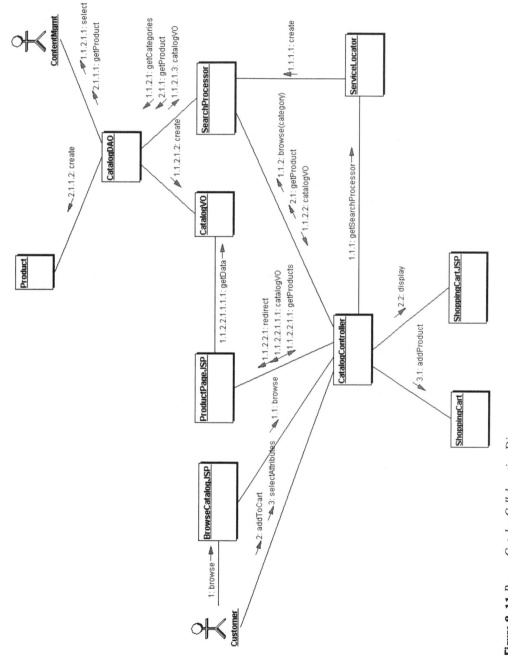

Figure 8-11 *Browse Catalog Collaboration Diagram*

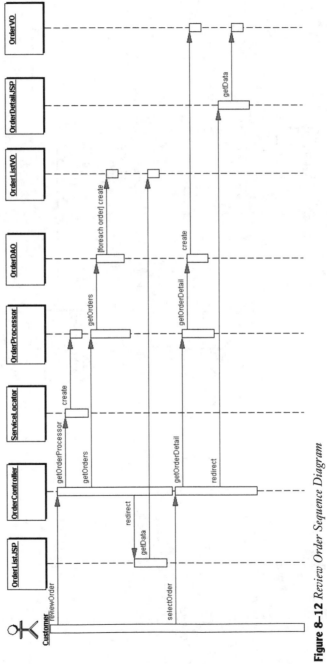

Figure 8–12 *Review Order Sequence Diagram*

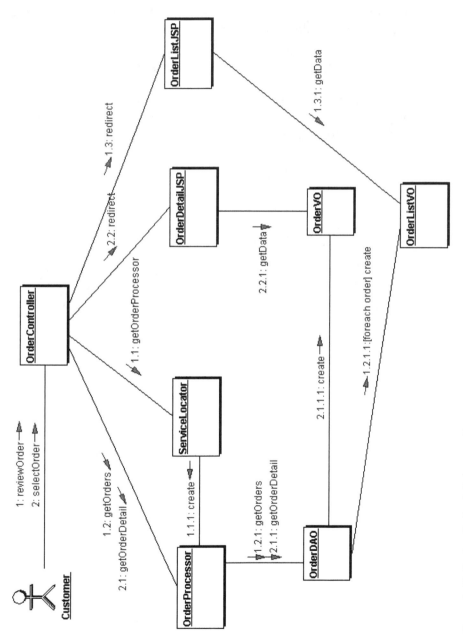

Figure 8–13 *Review Order Collaboration Diagram.*

8.3   Exam Part Three

When you have completed your assignment, you upload it for grading. After you have uploaded the assignment, you should schedule part three of the exam. When you complete part three of the exam, it gets merged with your assignment and sent to a grader. You get one combined grade for parts two and three. Part three is a series of short answer questions about your assignment. If you study for parts one and two and complete the assignment, then part three will be easy. Good luck on the exam and let us know how you fared.

A

Certification Success Guide

Java™ technology certification is a valuable, career-building opportunity—and a great way to help you take charge of your career. Sun Educational Services is behind you from the start with education, training, and the resources you need to help you reach your certification goals.

Sun Educational Services offers courseware and certification to support you in expanding your career opportunities and creating the systems and applications that fuel the future. The learning paths provide at-a-glance training and education information, so you know what you need to learn to successfully prepare for exams.

The Benefits of Certification

For The Individual

Becoming certified in Java technology can help you improve your career potential, gain more respect, and increase job security. With certification, you have hard evidence that you're qualified for the tasks that lie ahead, helping you increase your opportunities for professional advancement, such as salary increase, job role modifications, or promotions.

179

For The Corporation

Corporations that employ certified individuals do so to gain a competitive advantage. The skills that are verified during the certification process are the same skills that can help lead to decreased time to market, increased productivity, less system failure, and higher employee satisfaction rates.

Recruiting certified employees and certifying existing employees can lead to a more stable work environment, which in turn can lead to greater success as a whole. When companies demonstrate that they are willing to invest in their employees, those employees can be more productive, more loyal, and are more likely to remain in their jobs.

Certification Requirements Checklist

The Sun Certified Enterprise Architect for J2EE™ Technology is composed of three elements: a multiple-choice exam, an architecture and design project, and an essay exam.

You must successfully complete all three elements to become certified. The exam details are as follows:

STEP 1. SUN CERTIFIED ENTERPRISE ARCHITECT FOR J2EE TECHNOLOGY – MULTIPLE-CHOICE EXAM.

Available at: Authorized Prometric testing centers

Exam number: 310-051

Prerequisites: None

Exam type: Multiple choice, short answer, and drag and drop

Number of questions: 48

Pass score: 68%

Time limit: 75 minutes

Cost: US$150, or as locally priced

STEP 2. SUN CERTIFIED ENTERPRISE ARCHITECT FOR J2EE TECHNOLOGY – ARCHITECTURE AND DESIGN PROJECT.

Available at: My Certification database at http://suned.sun.com/US/certification/my_certification/index.html

Exam number: none

Prerequisites: Successful completion of the multiple-choice exam

Exam type: Architecture and design project

Number of questions: N/A

Pass score: 70%, subject to the evaluation of the essay exam and validation of the authenticity of the assignment

Time limit: None

Cost: As locally priced at the time of registration for the essay exam.

STEP 3. SUN CERTIFIED ENTERPRISE ARCHITECT FOR J2EE TECHNOLOGY – ESSAY EXAM.

Available at: Authorized Prometric testing centers

Examination number: 310-061

Prerequisites: Successful completion of the multiple-choice exam and submission of the architecture and design project

Exam type: Essay

Number of questions: 4

Pass score: N/A (please refer to the score in Step 1 above)

Time limit: 90 minutes

Cost: US$150, or as locally priced

Supporting Courseware

Our courseware offerings provide information to help you pass certification exams and do your job with confidence. For the Sun Certified Enterprise Architect for J2EE Technology, supporting courseware includes:

Architecting and Designing J2EE Applications

Course Number: SL-425

Duration: 4 days

Delivery: Instructor led

Steps to Certification

1. PREPARE FOR TESTING

Review the exam objectives in this guide to help verify that you have sufficient knowledge to complete them successfully.

2. VERIFY THE EXAM NUMBER AND REGISTER FOR THE MULTIPLE-CHOICE EXAM

When you're ready to register for the multiple-choice exam, you can purchase an exam voucher from your local Sun Educational Services office. To find your local office, go to http://www.sun.com/service/suned and choose the country in which you want to take the test.

3. CONTACT PROMETRIC TO SCHEDULE YOUR EXAM

The exam takes place at an authorized Prometric Testing Center. To register for a convenient date, time, and location, go to http://www.2test.com for information on your local Prometric office. In some countries, you may register for the exam online.

4. TAKE YOUR EXAMINATION

Before starting the exam, you must agree to maintain test confidentiality and sign the Certification Candidate Pre-Test Agreement, which can be viewed at http://suned.sun.com/US/certification/register/policies.html. If you do not sign the agreement, you will not be allowed to take the exam.

After completing your exam, you'll receive your score and a section-by-section assessment of your test performance. Your exam results will be available at http://suned.sun.com/US/certification/my_certification/index.html within three to five business days. If you do not pass the exam, you must wait two weeks before taking it again.

5. REGISTER FOR THE ARCHITECTURE AND DESIGN PROJECT

Once you've successfully completed the multiple-choice exam, you can purchase the architecture and design project from your local Sun Educational Services office. Within 24 hours, you'll be given permission to download the project. To find your local office, go to http://www.sun.com/service/suned and choose the country in which you want to register.

6. DOWNLOAD AND SUBMIT THE ARCHITECTURE AND DESIGN PROJECT

Go to My Certification database to download the architecture and design project at http://suned.sun.com/US/certification/my_certification/index.html.

Once you've completed the project, you can submit your work by uploading it to My Certification database.

7. VERIFY THE EXAM NUMBER AND REGISTER FOR THE ESSAY EXAM

After you've submitted the architecture and design project and you're ready to register for the essay exam, you can purchase an exam voucher from your local Sun Educational Services office. To find your local office, go to http://www.sun.com/service/suned and choose the country in which you want to take the test.

Once you've received the voucher, repeat steps three and four. You'll receive your score and performance feedback from the Sun Certification database at http://suned.sun.com/US/certification/my_certification/index.html within three to four weeks. If you do not pass, you may do the architecture and design project again and resubmit it for an additional US$150 fee (or as locally priced). You will not have to retake the essay exam.

After you've successfully completed all of the certification requirements, you'll receive a Welcome Kit from Sun, which includes a letter of congratulations, a personalized certificate, a lapel pin and a logo license agreement which, once signed, allows you to use the Java Technology logo on your business card. At that time, you might want to start thinking about the next certification in your professional future. To begin preparation, visit http://suned.sun.com/US/certification/to download the Certification Success Guide for the next certification in your career path.

Testing Objectives

Testing objectives for the Sun Certified Enterprise Architect for J2EE Technology include:

COMMON ARCHITECTURES

- Given an architecture described in terms of network layout, list benefits and potential weaknesses associated with it

LEGACY CONNECTIVITY

- Distinguish appropriate from inappropriate techniques for providing access to a legacy system from Java technology code given an outline description of that legacy system

ENTERPRISE JAVABEANS™

- List the required classes/interfaces that must be provided for an Enterprise JavaBean™ component
- Distinguish between stateful and stateless session beans
- Distinguish between session and entity beans
- Recognize appropriate uses for entity,s tateful session, and stateless session beans
- State the benefits and costs of container-managed persistence
- State the transactional behavior in a given scenario for an enterprise bean method with a specified transactional attributed as defined in the deployment descriptor
- Given a requirement specification detailing security and flexibility needs, identify architectures that would fulfill those requirements
- Identify costs and benefits of using an intermediate data-access object between an entity bean and the data resource

ENTERPRISE JAVABEANS™ CONTAINER MODEL:

- State the benefits of bean pooling in an Enterprise JavaBeans container
- Explain how the Enterprise JavaBeans container does lifecycle management and has the capability to increase scalability

PROTOCOLS:

- Given a list of some of its features, identify a protocol that is one of the following: HTTP, HTTPS, IIOP, or JRMP
- Given a scenario description, distinguish appropriate from inappropriate protocols to implement that scenario
- Select common firewall features that might interfere with the normal operation of a given protocol

APPLICABILITY OF J2EE™ TECHNOLOGY:

- Identify application aspects that are suited to implementation using J2EE technology
- Identify application aspects that are suited to implementation using Enterprise Java Beans
- Identify suitable J2EE technologies for the implementation of specified application aspects

DESIGN PATTERNS:

- Identify the most appropriate design pattern for a given scenario
- Identify the benefits of using design patterns
- State the name of a Gamma et al. design pattern given the UML diagram and/or a brief description of the pattern's functionality
- Identify benefits of a specified Gamma et al. design pattern
- Identify the Gamma et al. design pattern associated with a specified J2EE technology feature

MESSAGING:

- Identify scenarios that are appropriate to implementation using messaging, Enterprise JavaBeans technology, or both
- List benefits of synchronous and asynchronous messaging
- Identify scenarios that are appropriate to implementation using messaging
- Identify scenarios that are more appropriate to implementation using asynchronous messaging, rather than synchronous
- Identify scenarios that are more appropriate to implementation using synchronous messaging, rather than asynchronous

INTERNATIONALIZATION:

- State three aspects of any application that might need to be varied or customized in different deployment locales
- List three features of the Java programming language that can be used to create an internationalizable/localizable application

SECURITY:

- Identify security restrictions that Java 2 technology environments normally impose on applets running in a browser
- Given an architectural system specification, identify appropriate locations for implementation of specified security features and select suitable technologies for implementation of those features

Sample Questions

1. Which statement describes active replication for fault tolerance?

   A. Active replication requires all members to execute the same invocation.

   B. Active replication requires the master member to synchronize state with the slave members.

   C. Active replication requires the master member to notify the slave members for each invocation.

   D. Active replication requires the master member to send state to the fault tolerance backplane.

2. A shipping company is building an enterprise system to track the location of packages. One part of the tracking system is a network of wireless inventory devices. The devices can only be accessed using a custom, synchronous TCP/IP protocol. How should you encapsulate interaction with the wireless inventory system?

   A. with a Java class that uses a JMS to interact with the inventory system

   B. with a distributed CORBA object that uses IIOP to interact directly with the inventory system

   C. with an EJB™ stateful session bean that uses Java sockets to interact with the inventory system

D. with an EJB entity bean that uses container-managed persistence to encapsulate the inventory system

3. Which object can be used to increase cross-database and cross-schema portability?

A. entity bean

B. home object

C. session bean

D. data-access object

4. What are two features of HTTPS? (Choose two.)

A. It is secure.

B. It is connectionless.

C. It is connection-based.

D. It is used for load balancing.

E. It is used for remote object communications.

5. You are developing a system with the following requirements:

Users will access the system using a standard Web browser.

All incoming requests will be filtered based on the user's IP address.

The response to the request will be an appropriate static HTML page, based on the user's IP address.

Which two J2EE technologies should be used to handle HTTP requests? (Choose two.)

A. JSP

B. JTS

C. EJB

D. SNMP

E. servlets

6. What are two benefits of the Singleton pattern? (Choose two.)

A. It encourages use of global variables.

B. It controls access to a single instance.

C. It permits a variable number of instances.

D. It allows a collection of objects to be manipulated as a single object.

7. What is an advantage of asynchronous messaging?

   A. a simple architecture

   B. Components get an immediate response.

   C. Components are guaranteed delivery of a response.

   D. Components can make requests then perform tasks without waiting for a response.

8. Which two items explicitly support writing programs for international audiences? (Choose two.)

   A. int primitive type

   B. char primitive type

   C. java.lang.String class

   D. java.lang.Integer class

9. Which statement is true?

   A. Classes loaded into a browser from the local network are trusted.

   B. Classes loaded into a browser from remote sources are trusted if they are signed.

   C. Classes loaded into a browser from remote sources are trusted if they are in a signed jarfile.

   D. Classes loaded from a jarfile on a remote source can sometimes be trusted even if the jarfile is unsigned.

   E. Classes loaded from a signed jarfile are trusted if the public key associated with the jarfile's signature is marked as trusted in the keystore.

INDEX

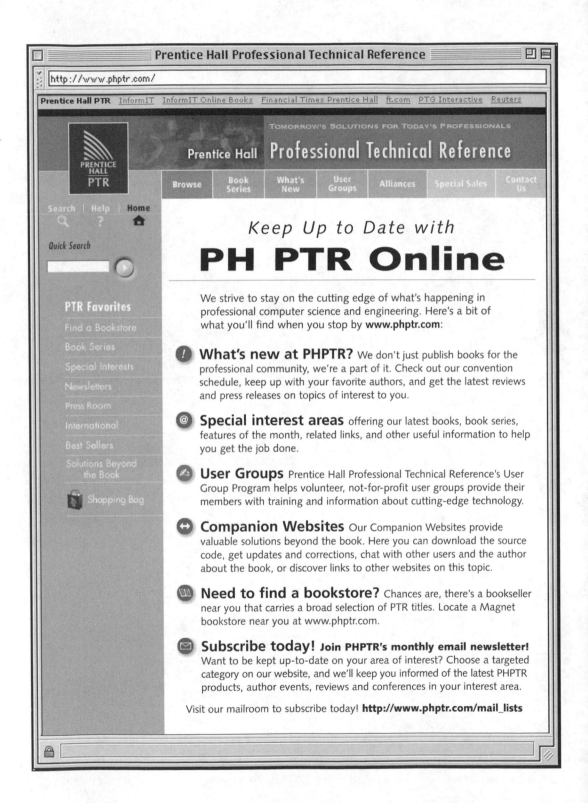

GET READY!

Congratulations on taking control of your career! With Sun certification, you can enjoy the benefits of increased job opportunities, greater career advancement potential, and more professional respect.

The first step in preparing for exams is discovering what you need to know. The next step is discovering what you don't. To help you measure your skills and understand any gaps, Sun offers online skills assessments. They'll help you focus your energies on learning the skills that can lead to certification. Online skills assessments are available at: http://suned.sun.com/USA/solutions/assessments.html.

GET SET!

Preparation is the key to success, and this study guide is a good first step. However, our years of experience have taught us that few people learn in exactly the same way. So we've created innovative learning solutions that can augment this guide, including:

Learning Solutions: Delivered via the Sun Web Learning Center, Sun's innovative eLearning solutions include Web-based training, online mentoring, ePractice exams, and the benefits of a community of like-minded people. Available by subscription, eLearning solutions from Sun give you anywhere, anytime learning—providing the flexibility you need to prepare according to your schedule, at your pace. You can visit the Sun Web Learning Center at http://suned.sun.com/WLC.

Practice Exams: Also available through the Sun Web Learning Center, ePractice exams are practice tools that can help you prepare for Sun's Java platform certifications. The questions in the ePractice exams are written in the same format as the certification tests, helping acquaint you with the style of the actual certification exams. You get immediate results and recommendations for further study, helping you prepare and take your certification tests with more confidence. You can register for ePractice exams at http://suned.sun.com/US/wlc/.

Instructor-Led Training: Sun's expert instructors provide unparalleled learning experiences designed to get you up to speed quickly. Available at over 200 Sun locations worldwide or at your facility, instructor-led courses provide learning experiences that will last a lifetime.

Self-Paced CD-ROM-based Training: Using JavaTutor, our CD-ROM-based learning solutions help you prepare for exams on your own terms, at your own pace, in a dynamic environment. After you're certified, they'll serve as perfect reference tools.

GO!

After you take your exams and become certified, go ahead and celebrate. For more information, visit: http://suned.sun.com.

Your road is wide open. Enjoy the journey.